THE LIGHT OF GLORY

THE LIGHT
OF GLORY

**READINGS FROM
JOHN DONNE
FOR LENT AND
EASTER WEEK**

EDITED BY
CHRISTOPHER L. WEBBER

MOREHOUSE PUBLISHING

Morehouse Publishing
P.O. Box 1321
Harrisburg, PA 17105

Morehouse Publishing is a division of Morehouse Group.

Cover design by Rick Snizik

Library of Congress Cataloging-in-Publication Data
Donne, John, 1572–1631.
  The light of glory : readings from John Donne for Lent and Easter week / edited by Christopher L. Webber.
      p. cm.
  Includes bibliographical references.
  ISBN 0-8192-1725-5 (pbk.)
  1. Lent—Prayer-books and devotions—English. 2. Eastertide—Prayer-books and devotions—English. I. Webber, Christopher. II. Title.
BV85.D62   1998
242'.34—dc21   97-34867
                                                                          CIP

Printed in the United States of America

10 9 8 7 6 5 4 3 2 1

Note: A study guide for this book is available on the Internet at
www.morehousegroup.com.

Contents

Introduction

About John Donne

When John Donne preached, it is said that children dropped their toys, old men crept from their corners, women fainted, and brave men wept.[1] However that may be, no other preacher in the English language has had so enduring a reputation and influence. That reputation rests on some 150 sermons that have come down to us, most of them preached during the brief ten years that Donne served as Dean of Saint Paul's Cathedral in London. Those were among the most peaceful years between the Reformation in the mid-sixteenth century and the Restoration of the monarchy in the latter part of the seventeenth century, but they were not completely quiet. John Donne was asked to defend the faith of the Church of England when the Gunpowder Plot of 1605 was still a vivid memory embittering relationships with the Church of Rome, and when the Puritans and Pilgrims were leaving England in despair to establish their own version of the Reformation in the New World. These controversies inevitably find a place in Donne's sermons, but a surprisingly small place under the circumstances. The focus instead is almost entirely on issues of personal faith: the certainty of death, the perils of sin, the mercy of God, the joy of redemption, the glory of heaven.

Donne was born in London in 1572. His mother was a member of a prominent Roman Catholic family, and Donne grew up in that faith. Graduating from Oxford, Donne read for the law but attempted to rise in the world of the royal court by winning the attention and support of influential patrons. Had he not married Ann More, the daughter of one such influential person—without her father's consent—he might have succeeded in his ambitions. As it was, he lost the progress he had made and found himself in his middle years with an ailing wife, a number of children, and no hope of obtaining the kind of position to which he had aspired. He had, however, attracted the king's notice with some essays in theology and been

---

[1] Webber, Joan. *Contrary Music: The Prose Style of John Donne* (Madison: University of Wisconsin Press, 1963), p. 90.

urged to pursue a career in the church. So it was that Donne turned to the study of theology and was ordained early in 1615, not long before his forty-third birthday.

Given the position of Divinity Reader of Lincoln's Inn the following year, Donne found himself in his element: using his skill with words to commend the Christian faith to the sort of ambitious young men among whom he had once been numbered. Five years later he was appointed Dean of Saint Paul's, the most influential pulpit in England. He died in 1631, after less than ten years in that position.

About the Readings

A certain reputation for emphasizing sin and death clings to Donne, perhaps because his best-known sonnet is about death and the best-known of his prose passages ends: "Send not to know for whom the bell tolls; it tolls for thee." Such an emphasis is certainly present in his writing, but it is more than balanced by equally eloquent passages about the joy and glory of heaven. "I would always raise your hearts... to a holy joy," he said in one sermon. In heaven, Donne said, "there is no darkness nor dazzling, but one equal light." His very human sermons, however, are full of the darkness of sin and the dazzling light of glory. He uses words not so much as to argue a point (though he did that tediously at times) as to paint pictures for his hearers. He asks them to ponder, to meditate, and he offers them shining pictures to take home in their hearts, more than in their minds. Such pictures easily make subjects for daily meditations in Lent. The emphasis on joy and heaven, however, made it seem less appropriate to end these readings with the last day of Lent than to continue through the first week of Easter season.

The readings selected for the weekdays are taken entirely from Donne's sermons. A poem and a prayer are provided for Sunday meditation. The series of daily readings begins with some thoughts on faith and repentance appropriate to the beginning of Lent. Then follows a series of meditations on our knowledge of God and on the human condition, on our knowledge of ourselves and of sin. These thoughts about sin are followed by meditations on repentance, forgiveness, and the mercy of God, and then, toward the middle of Lent, passages about joy and salvation. The fifth week of Lent is used for meditations on prayer and the church, while Holy Week begins with perhaps the darkest passage in all of Donne's sermons and two other passages on death and judgment. The last three days of Holy Week are assigned passages directly related to the events of those days, the Last Supper, the Crucifixion, and, on Easter Even, the meaning of baptism. The darkness of Holy Week leads then to Easter Week passages on Donne's favorite themes: mercy and joy and the light of heaven's glory.

About This Book

John Donne wrote in the first part of the seventeenth century, almost four hundred years ago, and the English language has changed greatly over that span of time. The language that was clear to the people of that day is not always clear to us. In addition, many people still knew the Latin Bible, so Donne could use Latin phrases and be understood. Language in our own time is still changing, rapidly in some respects. We have, for example, become aware of the way our language has been biased toward males, using masculine pronouns to refer to men and women alike and to refer to God, though God is beyond gender. Though inclusive language is important to some and not important to others, our language does seem to be moving in that direction; and it seems preferable therefore to use inclusive language wherever possible.

Taking all these factors into account, it has seemed best to revise Donne's passages and to present them as nearly as possible in contemporary English. The following principles have been adopted:

1. Biblical citations are from the New Revised Standard Version except where Donne's argument depends on the older wording, and that is indicated.
2. Obsolete words have been replaced.
3. Seventeenth-century English has been modernized (hath=has, thee=you, and so on).
4. Latin citations have been removed.

5. Passages have been condensed to focus more clearly on the main point.
6. Words have been altered to make the language inclusive.

This is not a scholar's edition of Donne. It is intended for ordinary church members and designed to be clear to the average reader. Donne labored to make himself clear to his hearers, and it seems likely that he would want his words to be clear to us.

When I began this work and thought of including some of Donne's poetry, I assumed the poems, at least, could not and should not be modernized. But when I showed some of them to people whose intelligence I respect and they asked, "What is that about?" I decided I should either attempt to clarify the poems or eliminate them. As a result, the poems, too, have been rewritten. For example:

Hath deign'd to chuse thee by adoption
Coheire to'his glory,'and Sabbath's endless rest.

becomes

And deigns to choose you by adoption
To be co-heir of glory and of rest.

Those who want to read Donne's poems in the original can easily find them. I hope those unfamiliar with his poetry and seventeenth-century English may be sufficiently intrigued by these revised versions to find the rest of his work in its original form.

Using This Book

For each day of Lent and Easter Week a passage is provided from the sermons of John Donne. On Sundays, one of the poems appears along with a brief prayer. The sources are given in a list at the back of the book. Each passage is focused clearly on one subject or one aspect of a subject, and is intended to provide material to think about during the day. At the end of each reading a few words from that passage are repeated as a mantra or handle to help provide a focus for the passage and to keep it in memory. Some may find it helpful to repeat these few words from time to time during the day.

Finally, readers will find more value in these readings as they spend time with them and connect them to their own lives. "The branches are many and full of fruit," said Donne in one of his sermons, "and I can but shake them and leave each one of you to gather your own portion, to apply those notes which may most advance your edification."

Acknowledgment

By the time this book is published, Allen Kelley, Publisher, and Deborah Graham, Editor, will have left Morehouse Publishing to move on to the next phase of their lives. For many years they have used their skills to provide the church with the best books and other materials for Christian development and have given generous support and encouragement to authors like myself. In this time of transition, I would like to express my gratitude to them for their years of dedicated ministry and service.

God Seeks for You

I love those who love me, and those who seek me diligently find me.
—Proverbs 8:17

There is no life without faith, nor any such life as constitutes righteousness without a personal faith of our own.

Consider how early God sought you. It is a great mercy that God waits so long for you. It was a greater mercy to seek you so early. Do you not feel that God seeks you now in offering love and asking yours? Can you not remember that God sought you yesterday, that is, that some temptations besieged you then and God sought you out by grace and preserved you? And has not God sought you so, so early, as from the beginning of your life? No, do you not remember that after you had committed that sin, God sought you by imprinting some remorse, some apprehension of God's judgments, and so by a miraculous and powerful working of God's spirit, God threatened you when God comforted you, God loved you when God chided you, God sought you when God drove you away?

God has sought you among the infinite numbers of false and fashionable Christians so that you might be brought out from the hypocrites to serve God in earnest, and in holiness and in righteousness. God sought you before that among the herd of the nations and Gentiles who had no church to bring you into God's enclosures and pastures, God's visible Church, and to feed you with God's word and sacraments. God sought you before that in the catalogue of all God's creatures where God might have left you simply as a stone or a plant or a beast. And then God gave you an immortal soul capable of all God's future blessings.

Yes, before this God sought you when you were nowhere, nothing. God brought you then, the greatest step of all, from being nothing to being a creature. How early did God seek you when you were still in Adam and out of that sour loaf in which we were all kneaded up, out of that condemned lump of dough, God sought and severed out that grain which you would be.

Yes, millions of millions of generations before all this God sought you in God's own eternal decree, and in that first scripture, which is as old as God, in the Book of Life, wrote your name in the blood of that Lamb which was slain for you, not only from the beginning of this world, but from the writing of that eternal decree of your salvation. So early God sought you in the church among hypocrites, out of the church among the heathen, in God's creatures among creatures of an ignoble nature, and in the first emptiness, when you were nothing, God sought you so early as in Adam, so early as in the Book of Life. And when will you think it a fit time to seek God?

When will I seek God?

Repentance

The saying is sure and worthy of full acceptance, that Christ Jesus came into the world to save sinners—of whom I am the foremost.
> —1 Timothy 1:15

Those who fall but yet believe, who fall and have a sense of their fall, are reserved by God's purpose to come by repentance to salvation. For those who fall thus, do not fall so desperately as to feel nothing between hell and themselves, nothing to stop at, nothing to check them on the way. They fall upon something. They do not fall upon flowers to wallow and tumble in their sin, nor on feathers to rest and sleep in their sin, nor into a cooling river to play and refresh and strengthen themselves in their sin, but they fall upon a stone where they may receive a bruise, a pain upon their fall, a remorse for that sin that they have fallen into.

They fall as a piece of money falls into a river. We hear it fall and we see it sink, and by and by we see it deeper, and at last we see it not at all. So no one falls at first into any sin without hearing their own fall. There is a tenderness in every conscience at the beginning, at the entrance into a sin, and they see for awhile the degrees of sinking also. But at last they are out of their own sight, until they meet this stone. This stone is Christ. That is, at last they meet some hard rebuke, some hard passage of a sermon, some hard judgment in a prophet, some cross in the world, something from the mouth or from the hand of God that breaks them. They fall on the stone and are broken.

To be broken upon this stone is to come to this sense, that though our integrity is lost, though we are no longer whole and complete vessels, yet there are means of piecing us together again. Though we are not vessels of innocence (for who is that?), yet we may be vessels of repentance acceptable to God and useful in God's service.

Those who feel their own fall upon this stone shall never feel this stone fall upon them. Those who come to a remorse early and earnestly after a sin and seek their reconciliation to God in the church are in the best position that anyone can be in now. For though we cannot say that repentance is as happy a position as innocence, yet certainly every particular human being feels more comfort and spiritual joy after a true repentance for a sin than they had in that innocence which they had before they committed that sin. Therefore in this case we may safely repeat those words of Saint Augustine, "I am bold to say that many a person has been the better for some sin."

...joy after a true repentance...

Feed Your Own Soul

Then Jacob woke from his sleep and said, "Surely the Lord is in this place—and I did not know it!" And he was afraid and said, "How awesome is this place! This is none other than the house of God, and this is the gate of heaven."
—Genesis 28:16–17

When we shall come to give an account of our stewardship, when we shall not measure our inheritance by acres for all heaven shall be ours and we shall follow the Lamb wherever he goes, when our estate and term shall not be limited by years and lives, but, as we shall be in the presence of the ancient of days, so our days shall be so equal that they shall be without end, then our great merchants, great producers, great contractors will find another language, another style, than they have been accustomed to here. There no one shall be called good security except the one who has made sure of their salvation. No one shall be called a careful merchant but the one who sold all to buy the pearl. No one shall be called a great officer except the one who desires to be a door keeper in the realm of heaven.

Now, everyone has a key to this door of heaven; everyone has some means to open it. Everyone has an oil to anoint this key and make it turn easily. All may go with more ease to heaven than to hell. Everyone has some means to pour this oil of gladness and comfort into another's heart. No one can say, "Lord, what have I to give you?" For everyone has something to give God: money, or labor, or counsel, or prayers. Everyone can give, and those who give to others in need for God's sake give to God. Do not ask, "When did we see you hungry or sick or in prison and did not minister to you?" (St. Matthew 25:44). Do not ask, "What can I do whose soul lacks so much?" For then God may come to that silence and weariness of asking at your hands to say, as it says in the psalm, "If I were hungry, I would not tell you" (Psalm 50:12). Then, although God has given you abundance, although God's children lack, yet God will not tell you, will not ask at your hands, will not enlighten your understanding, will not arouse your charity, will not give you any opportunity to do good with that which God has given you.

But God has given you a key. Yes, as God says to the Church of Philadelphia, "Look, I have set before you an open door, which no one is able to shut" (Revelation 3:8). You have the gate into heaven in yourself. If you are not aware of others' poverty and distress, yet have mercy on your own soul. You have a poor guest, an inmate, a sojourner within these mud walls, this corrupt body of yours. Be merciful and compassionate to that soul. Clothe that soul which is stripped and left naked of all its original righteousness. Feed that soul which you have starved. Purge that soul which you have infected. Warm and thaw that soul which you have frozen with lack of devotion. Cool and quench that soul which you have inflamed with licentiousness. Begin with your own soul; be charitable to yourself first and you will remember that God has made all humanity of one blood. Then you will find yourself in everyone in need and you will find Christ Jesus himself in them all.

Begin with your own soul...

Let Christ Come

The saying is sure and worthy of full acceptance, that Christ Jesus came into the world to save sinners—of whom I am the foremost.

—1 Timothy 1:15

At least be sure that Christ has come far enough into the world that he has come to you. You are a little world, a world a few spans long, and yet Christ was carried more quickly from east to west, from Jerusalem to these parts, than you can carry him into your soul and body. He has been on a pilgrimage toward you a long time, coming toward you perhaps fifty, perhaps sixty years, and how far as he got into you yet? Has he yet come to your eyes? Have they made Job's covenant, that they will not look upon a maid? (Job 31:1). Has he yet come into your ear? You still have an itching ear, delighting in the libelous defamation of others. Has he come to your ear? Are you corrected in that sense and yet still have longings in your taste or in your other senses and keep him out in those? Christ has come into your mouth, to your tongue, but Christ Jesus is in your mouth in blasphemies which would be earthquakes to us if we were earth. But we are all stones and rocks, hardened to a senselessness of those wounds which are inflicted on our God. Christ may have come to the outskirts, to the borders, to an outward evidence in your actions, and yet not have come into the land, into your heart.

Christ entered into you at baptism. He has crept farther and farther into you in catechisms and other infusions of his doctrine into you. He has pierced into you deeper by the powerful threatenings of his judgments, in the mouths of his messengers. He has made a survey of you in bringing you to call yourself to account for some sinful actions, and yet Christ has not come into you.

Perhaps you made some new discoveries and fell into some new ways of sin, and are reluctant that Christ should come to you yet, that he should trouble your conscience in that sin until you have made some profit from it. You have studied and must gain. You have bought and must sell. Therefore you are reluctant to be troubled yet. Or else you have some land within you which you yourself have never discovered, some ways of sin which you have never realized nor considered to be sin, and Christ has not come there yet. Christ has not come into you with that comfort which belongs to his coming unless he has overshadowed you all and is in you entirely.

Has Christ come to you?

The First Sunday in Lent

Will you love God as God loves you? Digest,
My soul, this wholesome meditation:
How God the Spirit, by angels waited on
In heaven, makes a temple in your breast;
The Father, who begot a Son most blest,
Does still beget (God never had begun)
And deigns to choose you by adoption
To be co-heir of glory and of rest.
And as one robbed may make a search and find
The stolen sold, and lose or buy again,
The Son of Glory came and here was slain
That we whom Satan stole he might unbind.
'Twas much that we were made like God before,
But that God should be made like us much more.

Prayer

O eternal and most glorious God,
sometimes in your justice
you give the dead bodies of the saints
to be meat for the birds of the heaven,
and the flesh of your saints
to the beasts of the earth,
so that their blood is shed like water,
and there is none to bury them;
sometimes you sell your people for nothing,
and do not increase your wealth by their price,
and yet you never leave us without the knowledge
that precious in your sight
is the death of your saints;
enable us,
in life and death,
seriously to consider the value,
the price of a soul;
It is precious, O Lord, because your image is stamped on it;
precious because the blood of your Son was paid for it;
precious because your Holy Spirit works on it;
precious because it is made a part of your treasure;
Do not allow us, therefore, so to undervalue ourselves,
or so to impoverish you, as to give away those souls,
those dear and precious souls, for nothing,
and all the world is nothing
if the soul must be given for it.

Now We See in a Mirror

Now we see in a mirror, dimly, but then we will see face to face. Now I know only in part; then I will know fully, even as I have been fully known.
—1 Corinthians 13:12

Our sight of God in this world, says our Apostle, is "in a mirror." But how do we see in a mirror? Truly that is not easily determined. But just as what we see in a mirror assures us that such a thing exists (for we cannot see a dream in a mirror, nor a fancy, nor a chimera), so this sight of God, which our Apostle says we have "in a mirror," is enough to assure us that there is a God.

This mirror reflects better than water; the water gives a crookedness and false dimension to things, as we see by an oar when we row a boat. But in the mirror of nature we may see directly that there is a God. It is a true sight of God, though it is not a perfect sight which we have this way. This theater where we sit to see God is the whole realm of nature; our medium, our mirror in which we see God, is the creation; and our light by which we see God is natural reason.

Aquinas calls this theater where we sit and see God the whole world. And the psalmist encompasses the world and finds God everywhere, and says at last, "Where can I flee from your presence? If I ascend to heaven, you are there" (Psalm 139:7–8). At Babel they thought they would build to heaven, but did anyone ever pretend to get above heaven, above the power of the winds, or above the dangerous orbits of meteors; can anyone get above the power of God? "If I take the wings of the morning and settle at the farthest limits of the sea, even there your hand shall lead me, and your right hand shall hold me fast" (Psalm 139:9–10).

If we sail to the waters above the firmament, it is so too. Nay, take a place which God never made, a place which grew out of our sins; that is hell; yet, "if I make my bed in Sheol, you are there" (Psalm 139:8). In a word, whether we are in the Eastern parts of the world or the Western, whether we are in the darkness of ignorance or the darkness of the works of darkness, or darkness of oppression of spirit, in sadness, the world is the theater that represents God, and everywhere, everyone may, no must, see God.

...everyone must see God.

The Light of Reason

Now we see in a mirror, dimly, but then we will see face to face. Now I know only in part; then I will know fully, even as I have been fully known.
—1 Corinthians 13:12

The whole frame of the world is the theater and every creature the stage, the medium, the mirror in which we may see God. There is no creature so poor that it cannot be the mirror to see God in. If every gnat that flies were an archangel, it could still only tell me that there is a God, and the poorest worm that creeps tells me that. The cedar is no better mirror to see God in than the hyssop on the wall. All things that are, are equally removed from being nothing; and whatever has any being is by that very being a mirror in which we see God, who is the root and fountain of all being. The whole frame of nature is the theater, the whole volume of creatures is the mirror, and the light of reason is our light.

If we say only that this light is the light of natural reason which, without question, "enlightens everyone who comes into the world" (St. John 1:9), still we have light enough to see God by that light, in the light of nature and in the mirror of creation.

God affords no one the comfort, the false comfort, of atheism. God will not allow pretending atheists the ability to think seriously that there is no God. They must pull out their own eyes and see no creature before they can say that they see no God. They must be no human being and quench their reasonable soul before they can say to themselves that there is no God. Atheists will pretend to know that there is no God, but they cannot say that they know that they know it because their knowledge will not stand up against the battering of another's argument, nor of their own reasoning. They dare not ask themselves, Who is it that I pray to in a sudden danger, if there is no God? No, they dare not ask, Who is it that I swear by in a sudden passion, if there is no God? Whom do I tremble at and sweat under at midnight, if there is no God?

And so for the sight of God that the Apostle offers here, which is to see that there is a God, the frame of nature, the whole world is our theater, the Book of Creatures is our medium, our mirror, and natural reason is light enough.

...reason is light enough.

Reason Must Be Satisfied

He himself was not the light, but he came to testify to the light.
—John 1:8

Human reason must be satisfied. But the method of such satisfaction must be this: to make us see that this world, a structure of so much harmony, so much elegance of style and convenience, must necessarily have had a builder, for nothing can make itself. We must see that no such builder would deliver a frame and work of so much majesty to be governed by fortune, casually, but would still retain the administration in the builder's hands. We must see that if the builder does this, makes the world, and sustains it by a watchful providence, then a worship and service belong to the builder for doing so. We must see, therefore, that the builder has certainly revealed to the human race what kind of worship and service will be acceptable. We must see that this manifestation of the builder's will must be permanent, it must be written, that there must be a scripture which is the builder's word and will. And we must see, therefore, that from that scripture, that word of God, all the articles of our faith are to be drawn.

If then our reason, admitting all this, asks further proof, to know how we shall understand that these scriptures accepted by the Christian Church are the true scriptures, let them bring any other book which pretends to be the word of God and compare it with these. It is true that we have no demonstration, no such evidence as that one and two are three, to prove these to be scriptures of God. God has not proceeded in that manner to drive our reason into a corner and force it by a complete necessity to accept these for scriptures, for then there would be no exercise of our will and our assent, if we could not have resisted. But yet these scriptures are so orderly, so sweet, so powerful a working on the reason and the understanding that any third person, with no preconceptions and anticipations in matters of religion, one who is altogether impartial and would weigh the evidence of the majesty of style, the harmony of the four evangelists, the consent and unanimity of the Christian Church ever since, and many other such reasons, that person would be drawn to such a historical, such a grammatical, such a logical belief of our Bible as to prefer it to all others that might claim to be the word of God. That person would believe it and would know the reason for it. For let no one think that God has given us so much ease here as to save us by believing we know not what or why.

Knowledge cannot save us, but we cannot be saved without knowledge. Faith is not on this side of knowledge but beyond it. We must necessarily come to knowledge first, though we must not stay in it when we come to it.

Many people walk by the seaside and the same beams of the sun give light to them all, but one gathers light pebbles or speckled shells for curious vanity by the benefit of that light while another gathers precious pearls or medicinal amber by the same light. So the common light of reason illumines us all, but one employs this light in the search for impertinent vanities, and others by a better use of the same light find out the mysteries of religion, and when they have found them, love them, not for the light's sake but for the natural and true value of the thing itself.

Faith is beyond knowledge...

The Church Is Our School

Now we see in a mirror, dimly, but then we will see face to face. Now I know only in part; then I will know fully, even as I have been fully known.
—1 Corinthians 13:12

The place where we take our degrees in the knowledge of God, our school, our university, is the Church. For though there may be a few examples of individuals who have grown learned who never studied at a university, so there may be some examples of individuals enlightened by God and yet not within the Church. Yet the ordinary place for degrees is the university and the ordinary place for illumination in the knowledge of God is the Church. One wall does not make a house; one opinion does not make catholic doctrine; one individual does not make a Church. For the knowledge of God, the Church is our school; there we must be bred and there we may be bred all our lives and yet learn nothing. Therefore, as we must be there, so there we must use the means, and the means in the Church are the Ordinances, and institutions of the Church.

The most powerful means is the scripture, but the scripture in the Church. Not that we are discouraged from reading the scripture at home: God forbid we should think any Christian family to be out of the Church. At home the Holy Spirit is with you in the reading of the scriptures, but as a remembrancer. ("The Holy Spirit will remind you of all that I have said to you," says our Savior [St. John 14:26].) Here in the Church the Spirit is with you as a Doctor to teach you. First learn at Church and then meditate at home. Receive the seed by hearing the scriptures interpreted here and water it by returning to those places at home. So then, your means are the scriptures. That is your evidence. But then this evidence must be sealed to you in the sacraments and delivered to you in preaching, and so sealed and delivered to you in the presence of competent witnesses, the congregation. When Saint Paul was carried up in an ecstasy "into Paradise" (2 Corinthians 12:4), it is not said that he saw, but that he heard unspeakable things. The eye is the devil's door before the ear, for, though the devil enters the ear by malicious speech, yet the devil was at the eye before. We see before we talk dangerously. But the ear is the Holy Spirit's first door. The Spirit assists us with ritual and ceremonial things which we see in the Church, but ceremonies have their right use when their right use has first been taught by preaching. Therefore the Apostle applies faith to hearing. And, as the Church is our school and our medium is the Ordinances of the Church, so the light by which we see this, that is know God and make God our own, is faith.

...the Church is our school.

Better Than Faith

Now we see in a mirror, dimly, but then we will see face to face. Now I know only in part; then I will know fully, even as I have been fully known.

—1 Corinthians 13:12

Though we know by faith, it is only a little that we know of a great deal. Faith is good evidence, but "the evidence of things not seen"(Hebrew 11:1). There is better evidence of them when they are seen. For we cannot believe as much of God, nor of our happiness in God, as we shall see then. The best knowledge that we have of God here, even by faith, is that God knows us, more than that we know God. And in this text, it is his own experience that the Apostle cites as an example, "Now I (I, an Apostle, taught by Christ himself) know but in part." And therefore, as Saint Augustine says, "The love which we bear to our neighbor is only the infancy, only the cradle of that love which we bear to God. So that sight of God which we have in nature, is only the infancy, only the cradle of that knowledge which we have in faith, is only the infancy and cradle of that knowledge which we shall have when we see God face to face."

Faith is infinitely above nature, infinitely above works, even above those works which faith itself produces, as parents are to children and the fruit is to the tree. But still faith itself is just as much below vision and seeing God face to face. And therefore, though we ascribe willingly to faith more than we can express, still let no one think they are so infallibly safe because they find that they believe in God as they shall be when they see God. The most faithful person in the Church must say "Lord, increase my faith." Whoever is least in the realm of heaven will never be put to that. All the world is only a mirror in which we see God. The Church itself and what the Ordinance of the Church brings to birth in us, faith itself, is but a dark representation of God to us, till we come to that state, "to see God face to face, and to know as we are known."

✳ ✳ ✳

…increase my faith.

The Light of Heaven

Now we see in a mirror, dimly, but then we will see face to face. Now I know only in part; then I will know fully, even as I have been fully known.

—1 Corinthians 13:12

For the sight of God here, our theater was the world, our medium and mirror was the creation, and our light was reason. For our knowledge of God here, our school was the Church, our medium the Ordinances of the Church, and our light the light of faith. So we consider the same terms, first for the sight of God and then for the knowledge of God in the next life.

First, the sphere, the place where we shall see God, is heaven. Those who ask me what heaven is do not mean to hear me but to silence me; they know I cannot tell them. When I meet them there I shall be able to tell them, and then they will be just as able to tell me. We shall be able to tell one another that this, this that we enjoy, is heaven, but the tongues of angels, the tongues of glorified saints, shall not be able to express what that heaven is, for even in heaven our faculties shall be finite. And in that place, where there are more suns than there are stars in the firmament (for all the saints are suns), and more light in another sun, the sun of righteousness, the Son of Glory, the Son of God, than in all that effusion of beams of glory, which began to shine not six thousand years ago, but six thousand millions of millions before that, in those eternal, in those uncreated heavens, we shall see God.

The light of glory is such a light that the one who sees any of it sees all of it, and so the light of glory is communicated entirely to every blessed soul. God made light first, and three days later that light became a sun, a more glorious light. God gave me the light of nature when I quickened in my mother's womb, by receiving a reasonable soul. And God gave me the light of faith when I quickened in my second mother's womb, the Church, by receiving my baptism. But in my third day, when my mortality shall put on immortality, God shall give me the light of glory, by which I shall see God's own self. Compared to this light of glory the light of honor is only a glow worm; the majesty itself only a twilight; the cherubim and seraphim are only candles; and that gospel itself, which the Apostle calls the glorious gospel, is only a star of the least magnitude. And if I cannot tell what to call this light by which I shall see it, what shall I call that which I shall see by it, the essence of God's own being? And yet there is something else than this sight of God intended in that which remains. I shall not only "see God face to face," but I shall "know" God (which, as you have seen, is above sight) and "know God, even as also I am known."

✳ ✳ ✳

I shall see God…

The Second Sunday in Lent

Batter my heart, three-personed God, for you
Now merely knock, breathe, shine, and seek to mend;
That I may rise, Lord, humble me and bend
Your force to break, blow, burn, and make me new.
I, like a conquered town to another due,
Strive to admit you, but Oh, to no end;
Reason your agent in me, should defend
Me, but is captive and proves weak, untrue.
Dearly I love you and would be loved fain
But am betrothed unto your enemy.
Divorce, untie, or break that knot again,
Take me to you, imprison me, for I
Unless you enthrall me never shall be free,
Nor ever chaste unless you ravish me.

Prayer

You alone, O Lord,
steer our boat through all our voyage,
but you have a more special care of it,
a more watchful eye on it,
when it comes to a narrow current
or to a dangerous fall of waters;
You have a care of these bodies of ours
in all the ways of our life;
But in the straits of death, open your eyes wider
and enlarge your providence toward us,
whether you are pleased to change our feathers into flakes
by withdrawing the conveniences of this life,
or to change our flakes into dust,
even the dust of the grave
by withdrawing us out of this life;
And though you divide husband and wife,
mother and child, friend and friend,
by the hand of death,
yet send away those who go with this consolation:
that though we part on many days and by many ways here
yet we shall all meet in one place and on one day,
a day that no night shall end,
the day of the glorious resurrection;
Hasten that day, O Lord,
for your Son Jesus Christ's sake.

A Love Like God's Love

Now we see in a mirror, dimly, but then we will see face to face. Now I know only in part; then I will know fully, even as I have been fully known.

—1 Corinthians 13:12

And then, what is it "to know God as we are known"? A comprehensive knowledge of God it cannot be. To comprehend is to know a thing as well as that thing can be known; and we can never know God so well that God will not still know more. Our knowledge cannot be expanded, nor God condensed and contracted so much that we can know God that way, comprehensively. It cannot be such a knowledge of God as God has of God's own being, nor as God has of us; for God comprehends us and all this world and all the worlds that could have been made and God's own nature. As God knows me, so shall I know God; but I shall not know God as God knows me. It is not "as much" but "as truly." The fire shines as truly as the sun shines, but it does not shine so far or to as many purposes. So then I shall know God with nothing in me to hinder my knowing, which cannot be said of human nature, even regenerate, on the earth, no, nor of the nature of an angel in heaven, left to itself, until both have received a superillumination from the light of glory. And then it shall be a knowledge so like God's knowledge that it shall produce a love like God's love, and we shall love God as God loves us. If God could be seen and known in hell, hell in an instant would be heaven. And as this seeing and knowing of God crowns all other joys and glories, even in heaven, so this very crown is crowned. There grows from this a higher glory which is that we "may become participants of the divine nature"

(2 Peter 1:4)—immortal as the Father, righteous as the Son, and full of comfort as the Holy Spirit.

Let me dismiss you with an easy request of Saint Augustine: simply love yourselves. That person does not love God who does not love self. Simply love yourselves. For if you love God, you would live eternally with God, and if you desire that, and attempt it earnestly, you do truly love yourself, and not otherwise. And you love God if, by seeing God in the theater of the world, and in the mirror of creation, by the light of reason, and knowing God in the school of the Church, by its Ordinances, through the light of faith, you endeavor to see God in heaven, through the light of glory, and to know God as God is all in all. You do this contemplatively by knowing as you are known. You do it practically by loving as you are loved.

Love yourself…

Creation

Then God said, "Let us make humankind in our image, according to our likeness; and let them have dominion over the fish of the sea, and over the birds of the air, and over the cattle, and over all the wild animals of the earth, and over every creeping thing that creeps upon the earth."

—Genesis 1:26

Never was such a building so soon set up as this, in this chapter. "In the beginning God created the heavens and the earth" (Genesis 1:1), that earth which no one is ever said to have compassed till our age, that earth which is too much for us yet, for as yet a very great part of the earth is unpeopled, that earth which, if we will make it all into a map, costs many months' labor to engrave it. Nay, if we will cast but a piece of an acre of it into a garden, it costs many years' labor to fashion and furnish it. All that earth and then that heaven which spreads so far that scholars have with some appearance of probability imagined that in that heaven, in those manifold spheres of the planets and the stars, there are many earths, many worlds, as big as this which we inhabit. That earth and that heaven which God, Almighty God, spent six days in furnishing, the Bible sets up in a few syllables, in one line: "In the beginning God created heaven and earth."

If one of our extensive and voluminous authors had a hand in this story, God would have had to make another world to have made a library to hold the author's books on the making of this world. It may assist our imagination to consider that among those authors who proceed with a sober modesty and limitation in their writing and let their conscience stop them from clogging the world with unnecessary books, still the volumes which they have written about this beginning of Genesis are scarcely less than infinite. God merely said, let this and this be done. And the Bible merely says that when God spoke, it was done.

Only, beloved, remember that a frame may be thrown down in much less time than it was set up. A child, an ape, can give fire to a cannon, and a vapor can shake the earth, and these fires and vapors can throw down cities in minutes. When Christ said, "Destroy this temple, and in three days I will raise it up" (St. John 2:19), they never hesitated concerning throwing it down. They knew that might be soon done, but they wondered at the speedy raising of it.

Now, if all this earth were made in that minute, may not all come to the general dissolution in this minute? Or may not your acres, your miles, your counties shrink into feet, and so few feet as shall make up only your grave? Those who are in it become the same earth that they lie in. They all make but one earth and but a little of it. But then raise yourself to a higher hope again. God has made better land, the land of promise; a stronger city, the New Jerusalem; and inhabitants for that everlasting city whom God made, not by saying, let there be human beings, but on consultation, by deliberation: "God said let us make human beings in our image, after our likeness."

...when God spoke, it was done.

Human Life

Then God said, "Let us make humankind in our image, according to our likeness; and let them have dominion over the fish of the sea, and over the birds of the air, and over the cattle, and over all the wild animals of the earth, and over every creeping thing that creeps upon the earth."

—Genesis 1:26

We are but earthen vessels it is true, but God is the potter. If God will be that, I am well content to be this. Let me be anything, if what I am is from God. I am as well content to be a sheep as a lion, if God will be my Shepherd; and the Lord is my Shepherd; to be a cottage as a castle, if God will be the builder, and the Lord builds and watches the city, the House, this House, this city, me; to be rye as wheat, if God will be the farmer, and the Lord plants me and waters and weeds and gives the increase; and to be clothed in leather as well as in silk, if God will be the merchant, and God clothed me in Adam and assures me of clothing by clothing the lilies of the field and is fitting the robe of Christ's righteousness to me now, this minute.

You are earth. In the grave all dusts are equal. Unless an epitaph tells me who lies there, I cannot tell by the dust. Nor by the epitaph can I know which dust it speaks of if another has been laid before or after in the same grave. Nor can any epitaph be confident in saying, "Here lies"; but, "Here was laid." So transitory is all this world that even the dust of the grave has revolutions. The changes of this life work after death. And as envy removes us alive, a shovel removes us and throws us out of our grave after death. No measurement, no weights can tell you, this is royal dust, this plebeian dust. No commission, no inquisition can say, this is Catholic, this is heretical dust.

All lie alike, and all shall rise alike, at once, and on one command. The saint cannot accelerate, the sinner cannot retard the resurrection. And all that rise to the right hand shall be equally enthroned.

God made us all of earth and all of red earth. Our earth was red even when it was in God's hands, a redness that amounts to a blushing at our own infirmities is imprinted in us by God's own hand. For this redness is but a conscience, a guiltiness for needing a continual supply of more and more grace. And we are all red, red even from the beginning and in our best state. This redness, this blushing, is an acknowledgment that we could not exist with any measure of faith unless we pray for more faith, nor of grace unless we seek more grace from the hand of God. And we have another redness from God's hand too, the blood of God's Son, for that blood was poured out by Christ as a ransom for all and accepted by God for all. So we are red earth in the hands of God.

God made us all of red earth...

What Am I?

Then God said, "Let us make humankind in our image, according to our like-ness; and let them have dominion over the fish of the sea, and over the birds of the air, and over the cattle, and over all the wild animals of the earth, and over every creeping thing that creeps upon the earth."

—Genesis 1:26

We are only earth it is true, but earth is the center. Those who dwell on them-selves, who are always conversing with themselves, rest in their true center. We are celestial creatures too, heavenly creatures, and those who dwell upon themselves have their conversation in heaven. If you weigh anything in a scale, the greater it is, the lower it sinks. As you grow greater and greater in the eyes of the world, sink more and more in your own. If you ask yourself, "What am I?" and are able to answer yourself, "Why now I am a person of title, of honor, of place, of power, of possessions, one fit for a title, one known in the Herald's office," go to the Herald's office, the sphere and element of honor, and you shall find the people as busy there about the consideration of funerals as about titles. You shall find the office to be as much the grave, as the cradle of honor. And you shall find in that office as many records of fallen families, impoverished and forgotten and obliterated families, as of families newly raised and presently celebrated. Whatever height any of us may have at home, there is some other in some higher place than yours who weighs you down. And the one who stands in the highest supreme height in this world is weighed down by that which is nothing. For what is any monarch to the whole world? And the whole world is only that; only what? Only nothing.

What person among us who is named to any place by the good opinion of others or who calls on others and begs and buys their good opinion for that place begins like Moses by asking, "What am I? Where have I studied and practiced sufficiently that I should fill such or such a judgeship? What am I? Where have I served and labored and preached in inferior places of the church that I should fill such or such a place of dignity? What am I? Where have I seen and encountered and defeated the enemy that I should fill such or such a place of command in the army?"

There is no Abraham left to say, "O my Lord, I am but dust and ashes"; no Jacob left to say, "O my Lord, I am not worthy"; no David left to say, "O my Lord, I am but a dead dog and a flea." But everyone is vapored up into air and, as the air can, they think they can fill any place. Everyone is under that complicated disease which is not content with the most and yet is proud of the least, so when they look on others they despise them and when they look at God they murmur at God because God did not place them on the throne.

But if we will not come to ask, "Who am I?" God will come to ask, "Who are you?" and, "Friend, how did you come in here?" To all who come in by improper means, God will say, "What did you do to take my word into your mouth? What did you do to take my sword into your hand?" Only to those who are little in their own eyes shall God say, as Christ said to his Church, "Fear not, little flock, for it is your Father's good pleasure to give you the realm of heaven" (St. Luke 12:32).

What am I?

Why Am I Here?

He himself was not the light, but he came to testify to the light.
—St. John 1:8

How far are those wretched and sinful human beings from giving any testimony or glory to Christ in their life who never come to know and consider why they were sent into this life? Who are so far from doing their errand as those who do not know what the errand was or whether they received any errand or not? It is as if that God who for infinite millions of ages was sufficient alone and then bestowed six days' labor for the creation and provision of human kind, as if that God who, when we were poisoned in the fountain, withered in the root, would then engage God's Son, God's beloved Son, God's only Son, to become human by a brief life ended by a violent and a shameful death, as if that God, when pleased to begin to create, might have left you out among nothings or might have shut you up in the close prison of their being and no more, as God has done with earth and stones, or, if God had given you life, might have left you a toad, or, if God had given you a human soul, might have left you a heathen without any knowledge of God, as if that God who has done so much more in raising you in the church, had done all this for nothing so that you might pass through this world like a flash, like a lightning, whose beginning or end no one knows, and you might pass out of this world as your hand passes out of a basin of water, which may be somewhat the fouler for your washing in it but retains no other impression of your having been there, and so does this world for your life within it.

When God placed Adam and Eve in the world, God ordered them to fill it and subdue it and rule it. When God placed them in Paradise, God ordered them to dress and keep Paradise. God gives everyone some task, some errand for God's glory. And yet you come from God into this world as if God had said nothing to you but, "Go and do as you see fit; go and do as you see others do."

You do not know what you were sent to do, what you should have done, and you know even less what you have done. The light of nature has taught you to hide your sins from others and you have been so diligent in that that you have hidden them from yourself and cannot find them in your own conscience. You cannot find them out so that a sermon or sacrament can work upon them.

✳ ✳ ✳

...to everyone some errand for God's glory.

Accuse Yourself

He himself was not the light, but he came to testify to the light.
                                                  —St. John 1:8

By the light of faith and grace we may come to such a participation in the
light of heaven in this world that what was said of the Ephesians will be true
of us, "You were once darkness, but now in the Lord you are light." It does
not say "enlightened" or "light-giving" but light itself, light essentially, for
our citizenship is in heaven.

This is that glorification which we shall have at the last day. And we consider a great part of that glory to be the baring and manifestation of all to
all. In this world, a great part of our inglorious servitude is in those dis-
guises, those colors and pretenses of public good, with which those with
power and authority cloak their oppression of the poor. In this we are more
miserable because we cannot see their ends, because there is none of this
baring, this laying open of ourselves to one another, which shall accompa-
ny that state of glory where we shall see one another's bodies and souls,
actions and thoughts. And therefore, as if this place were now the tribunal
of Christ Jesus and this that day of judgment and openness, we must be here
as we shall be there, content to stand naked before him, content that there
be a discovery, a revealing, a manifestation of all our sins, at least to our own
conscience though not to the congregation. If we will have glory, we must
have this baring.

We must not be glad when our sins escape the preacher. We must not say
(as though there were a comfort in that), "Though he has hit such a one's
adultery, and another's ambition, and another's extortion, yet, for all his

diligence he has missed my sin." For if you would wish it to be missed, you would wish to hold it still. And then, why did you come here? Why did you come to church or to the sacrament? Why do you delude God with this ceremonial visit, to come to God's House, if you do not bring with you a disposition to God's honor and service? Did you come only to test whether God knew your sin and could tell you of it by the preacher? Alas, God knows it now infallibly, and if God brings no knowledge of knowing it to your conscience by the words of the preacher, your state is the more desperate.

God sends us to preach forgiveness of sins. Where we find no sin we have no commission to execute. How shall we find your sins? In the old sacrifices of the law the priest did not fetch the sacrifice from the herd, but received it from the one who brought it and so sacrificed it for them. Do you therefore prevent the preacher? Accuse yourself before you are accused. Offer up your sin yourself. Bring it to the top of your memory and your conscience, that the preacher finding it there may sacrifice for you. Remember your own sins first and then every word that falls from the preacher's lips shall be a drop of the dew of heaven, a portion of the blood of your Savior, to wash away that sin so presented by you to be so sacrificed by the preacher.

By our citizenship in heaven here, our watchfulness that we do not fall into sin, we have possession of heaven and of the light of God's presence and a beginning of our glorified state.

...we must have this baring.

The Third Sunday in Lent

Oh to vex me contraries meet in one:
Inconstancy unnaturally has begot
A constant habit so, when I would not,
I change in vows and in devotion.
As changeable is my contrition
As my profane love, and as soon forgot;
As puzzlingly disordered, cold and hot
As praying, as mute; as infinite as none.
I dared not view heaven yesterday, today
In prayers and flattering speeches I court God,
Next day I quake before God's chastening rod.
So my devout fits come and go away
Like a fantastic sickness, save that here
Those are my best days when I shake with fear.

Prayer

My sin, O God,
has not only caused your descent into this world
and your suffering here,
but by it I have become that hell
into which you descended after your death,
indeed after your glorification,
for hourly you descend in your Spirit into my heart
to overthrow there the legions of spirits
of disobedience and faithlessness and murmuring.
Yet, O God, have mercy on me,
for your own sake, have mercy on me,
Let not my sin frustrate your purposes,
But let me be of so much use to your glory
that by your mercy to my sin,
other sinners may see how much sin you can pardon
and so show mercy to many in one.
Hear us, O God, hear us,
For this contrition which you have put into us,
Who come to you with that watchword
By which your Son assured us of access:
    Our Father…

Hidden Sin

He himself was not the light, but he came to testify to the light.
—St. John 1:8

Perhaps you can tell when the first time was or where the first place was that you committed such or such a sin but in the same way as one can remember when they began to spell but not when they began to read perfectly, when they began to join their letters but not when they began to write perfectly. So you remember when you went surely and cheerfully about sin at first and now perhaps are ashamed of that shame and sorry you began no sooner. Poor bankrupt! You have sinned out your soul so profusely, so lavishly, that you dare not balance your accounts, you dare not ask yourself whether you have any soul left.

How far are you from giving any testimony to Christ if you dare not testify to yourself nor hear your conscience take knowledge of your friends' commissions, but would rather sleep out your days or drink out your days than leave one minute for regret to lay hold on you. You do not sin always for the love of that sin but for fear of a holy sorrow if you should not fill up your time with that sin. God cannot be mocked, says the Apostle, nor can God be blinded. God sees all the way, and at your last gasp God will make you see too. Can you hope that that God who sees this dark earth through all the vaults and arches of the spheres of heaven, that sees your body through all your stone walls and sees your soul through that which is darker than all those, your corrupt flesh, can you hope that that God can be blinded by drawing a curtain between your sin and God? When God is all eye, can you hope to put out that eye by putting out a candle? When God has planted legions of angels around you, can you hope that you have taken away all knowledge if you have corrupted or sold or sent away a servant? Oh, give as much labor to find out those sins in those corners where you have hidden them as you have done to hide them.

Bring this dawning and break of day to a full light and this little spark to a perfect acknowledgment of your sins. Go home with this spark of God's Spirit in you and look at your rentals and know your oppressions and extortions, look at your account books and know your deceits and falsifications, look in your wardrobe and know your excesses. Till then, till you come to this survey, this sifting of conscience, if we should cry peace, peace, yet there would be no peace.

We might flatter you and you would say we were sweet and smooth and comfortable preachers and we might perish together. If you study yourself, if you read your own history, if you get to the knowledge of your errand here and the poor discharge of those duties, the sorrow and regret which will grow for your sins will become a witness to your self of your reconciliation to God in the merits of Christ Jesus.

...study yourself.

Pride Is the First Sin

As he walked by the Sea of Galilee, he saw two brothers, Simon, who is called Peter, and Andrew his brother, casting a net into the sea—for they were fishermen. And he said to them, "Follow me, and I will make you fish for people." Immediately they left their nets and followed him.

—St. Matthew 4:18–20

The first act of those angels that fell was an act of pride. They did not thank or praise God for their creation. They did not pray to God to sustain them or improve them or strengthen them. But the first act that those first creatures did was an act of pride, a proud over-valuation of their condition. They imagined that they could stand by themselves without any further relationship or indebtedness to God. So early, so primary a sin is pride that it was the first act of the first of creatures.

So early, so primary a sin is pride that this first pride in the angels was a positive pride, but all sin now is comparative. No rulers think themselves great enough, yet they are proud that they are independent, sovereign, subject to none. No subjects think themselves rich enough, yet they are proud that they are able to oppress others who are poor. All these are only comparative prides; there must be some subjects to compare with before rulers can be proud and some poor before the rich can be proud. But the pride of those angels in heaven was a positive pride; before there was any other creature with whom those angels could compare themselves, those angels were proud of themselves. So early, so primary a sin is pride.

Solitude is not the scene of pride. The danger of pride is in company, when we meet to look upon another. How many have we known who have been content all the week at home alone with their work-a-day faces as well as with their work-a-day clothes, and yet on Sundays, when they come to church and appear in company, they will change both their faces and their clothes. Not solitude but company is the scene of pride.

So early, so primary a sin is pride that out of every mercy and blessing which God gives us, we gather pride. Indeed, we see even children striving for place and position, and mothers are ready to go to the Herald's office to know how cradles shall be ranked and which cradle shall have the highest place. And as our pride begins in our cradle, it continues in our graves and monuments. Persons whom the devil kept from church all their lives, pride and vain glory brings to church after their deaths in an expectation of high places and elaborate monuments in the church. And those who have given nothing at all to any pious use, in that one day of their funeral give large annuities for repainting their tombs and for new flags and decorations every certain number of years.

Oh the earliness! Oh the lateness! How early a spring and no autumn! How fast a growth and no decline of this branch of the sin of pride. This love of place and precedence rocks us in our cradles and lies down with us in our graves.

✳ ✳ ✳

...pride is the primary sin.

Hardness of Heart

Because sentence against an evil deed is not executed speedily, the human heart is fully set to do evil.

—Ecclesiastes 8:11

The hardest thing of all is for sinners to return to their own hearts and to find them after they have strayed and been scattered into many different sins. The holiest people cannot always find their own hearts. Their hearts may be set on religion and yet they cannot tell which religion, and on preaching and yet they cannot tell which preacher, and on prayer and yet they find themselves wandering in their prayer. How much harder is it to find the wandering and vagabond heart of an ordinary sinner by any search. If they ask for their heart where they remember it was yesterday involved in lascivious and lustful purposes, they shall hear that it went from there to some riotous feasting, from there to some blasphemous gambling, and after that to some malicious conspiracy for entangling one and supplanting another. They shall never trace it so well as to bring it home, that is, to a consideration of itself and that God who made it.

Be careful that these sins carry you no further than you intend. You intend only pleasure or profit, but the sin will carry you further. Do you ask where? To a numbness, a hardness of heart. Never ask what that hardness of heart is, for if you do not know, you have it. The fullness and so the incurableness of the heart comes by perpetual motion. Because sinners are in perpetual progress from sin to sin, they never consider their condition.

There is another fullness here when the sinner comes to a full consideration of the sin and a settledness in it on a foundation of reason, as though it were not only an excusable but even a wise proceeding. But when we become thus fully set, God shall set us fast. Our transgressions shall be sealed up in a bag and what is this bag of God, but the heart of that sinner? There, like a wretched miser's bag of money which shall never be opened, never counted till the miser's death, lies this bag of sin, this frozen heart of an impenitent sinner. And their sins shall never be opened, never told to their own conscience, till it be done to their final condemnation. God shall allow them to settle where they have chosen to settle themselves, in an unawareness of their own condition. But who can be more miserable than those who do not sympathize with their own misery? How far gone are they into a pitiful condition when they neither desire to be pitied by others nor pity themselves, nor understand that their condition needs pity?

Because the maledictions of God are honeyed and candied over with a little crust or sweetness of worldly ease, we do not understand them in their true taste and right nature. The jingling and rattling of our chains and fetters makes us deaf. The weight of the judgment takes away the sense of the judgment. This is the full setting of the heart to do evil, when we fill ourselves with the liberty of passing into any sin without concern.

...hard to return to our own hearts.

Cleansing Required

Abraham was ninety-nine years old when he was circumcised in the flesh of his foreskin.

—Genesis 17:24

The word "circumcision" here means purging, it means cleansing and purifying the conscience, and it means to cut down, weed, and root out whatever remains in our possession that was unjustly gotten.

A house is not clean even though all the dust be swept together, if it still lies in a corner indoors. A conscience is not cleansed by having recollected all its sins in the memory, for they may fester there and gangrene even to desperation until they are emptied into the bottomless sea of the blood of Christ Jesus and the mercy of his Father. But a house is not clean either, even though the dust be thrown out, if cobwebs hang about the walls and in any dark corners. A conscience is not clean, even though the sins brought to our memory are cast on God's mercy and the merits of God's Son, if there remains in me even a cobweb, a little but a sinful delight in the memory of those sins which I had formerly committed.

How many of us sin the sins of our youth again in our age by a sinful delight in remembering those sins and a simple desire that our bodies were not past them? How many of us sin over some sins in imagination (and yet damnably) a hundred times which we never sinned actually at all, by filling our imaginations with such thoughts as these: How would I have revenge on my enemy, if I were in a place of authority? How easily could I destroy such a wasteful person and gain their property, if I only had money to feed their vices? Those sins which we have never been able to do actually to the harm of others, we do as hurtfully to our own souls by a sinful desire for them and a sinful delight in them. There is, therefore, a cleansing required, such a cleansing as God promises: I will cleanse their blood of all corrupt desires and sinful delights.

Now there is no cleansing of our blood but by his blood, and the application of his blood is in the seal of the sacrament. So only that soul is cleansed that preserves itself always in, or returns speedily to, an inclination toward a worthy receiving of that holy and blessed sacrament. Those who are now in that disposition are the ones who dare to meet their Savior at that table and receive him there.

We must cut the root, the mother-sin that nourishes all our sins and the branches too. There must be a cutting down which is not done until we have shaken off all that we have gotten by those sins. It requires a cutting off of the root and branch, the sin and the fruits, the profits, of that sin. I must not imagine that I can bribe God by giving God some of the profit of my sin to let me enjoy the rest. Was God a venturer with me in my sin? Or did God send me to sea, that is, put me into this world, to see what I could get by usury, by oppression, by extortion, and then give God a part for charitable uses? As long as you make a profit or take pleasure in anything sinfully gotten, your sin grows. So this cleansing is not perfected except by restitution and satisfaction of all that was done.

✳ ✳ ✳

...we must cut the root.

True Confession

Then I acknowledged my sin to you, and I did not hide my iniquity; I said, "I will confess my transgressions to the Lord," and you forgave the guilt of my sin.
—Psalm 32:5

True confession is a mysterious art. And the mystery of the kingdom of heaven is this: that no one comes to it without being a notorious sinner. One mystery of this world is that although I may multiply sins, the judge cannot judge me if I hide them from others, even though the judge may know them. But if I confess them, the judge can and will and must judge me. The mystery of the realm of heaven is that only the declaring, publishing, and confessing of my sins gives me possession of the realm of heaven. There is a situation in which the notoriety of my sin both scandalizes others and tempts them, so that they acquire my sin by my example. And their sin becomes mine because I gave them the example. So we aggravate each other's sins and both of us sin both sins. But there is a publication of sin that both alleviates, indeed annihilates my sin, and makes God who hates sin love me better because I have confessed it. Therefore, we speak of the mystery of confession.

In this confession of David's [the psalm quoted above] there are two parts, David's act and God's act, confession and absolution, but there is more than one single action in each of them. In the first, there is a reflection that David makes with himself before he comes to his confession to God. What preceded his confession was "I acknowledged my sin." This is David's act within himself, the recalling and recollecting of his sins in his own memory. And then, finding the number and weight and oppression of those sins, he considers how he may rid himself of them. "I said I will confess," says David. I thought what was best to do and I resolved to do it and did it. These are the elements of his confession: he will confess sins, not flattering or holding back; he will acknowledge them to have been committed by himself; he will not blame them on anyone else, least of all God; and he will confess his own sins and not meddle in the sins of others.

God is the rock of our salvation. God is no occasional God, no accidental God, neither will God be served by occasion or by accident but by a constant devotion. Our communication with God must not be in interjections that come in by chance, nor our devotion made up of parentheses that might be left out. God is not destiny, for then there could be no reward or punishment. But God is not fortune either, for then there would be no providence. If God has given reason only to us, it would be strange if we should exercise that reason in our moral and civil actions and only do God's worship casually. Not to consider the nature of confession and absolution, not to consider the nature of the sins we should confess and the absolution of them is a stupidity different from what this text would indicate. The psalmist meditated, but then the psalmist resolved, and having resolved, did it.

…confessing my sins gives me heaven.

God Is an Early Riser

Satisfy us in the morning with your steadfast love,
so that we may rejoice and be glad all our days.
—Psalm 90:14

"Weeping may linger for the night," says another psalm (30:5). The psalm does not say it must endure for a night, that God will by no means shorten the time. Perhaps God will wipe away all tears from your eyes at midnight, if you pray. Try God that way then. But if weeping does "linger for the night," all night, yet "joy comes with the morning." And then it does not say, joy may come in the morning, but it comes certainly, it comes infallibly, and it comes in the morning. God is an early riser. This is God's promise, this is God's practice, this is God's pace.

Now if we look for this early mercy from God, we must rise early too and meet God early. Our life is a warfare, our whole life. It is not only with lusts in our youth and ambitions in our middle years and devotions in our age, but with agonies in our body and temptations in our spirit upon our deathbed that we are to fight. And those cannot be said to overcome who fight not out the whole battle. If you enter not the field in the morning, that is apply not yourself to God's service in your youth, if you continue not in the evening, if you faint in the way and grow remiss in God's service, God will overcome and God's glory will stand fast, but you can scarcely be said to have overcome.

It is the counsel of the wise man that "one must rise before the sun to give God thanks and must pray to God at the dawning of the light" (Wisdom of Solomon 16:28). Rise as early as you can; you cannot be up before God, no, nor before God raises you. However you rise before this sun, this sun of the firmament, yet the Son of heaven has risen before you, for without God's grace, you could not stir. Have any of you slept through your morning, resisted God's moving you to private prayer at home, neglected God's callings so? Though you do sleep through your morning, the sun goes on its course and comes to its noontime splendor, though you have not looked toward it. That sun which has risen to you at home, in that inward movement, has gone on its course and has shone out here in this house of God every day. All this, at home and here, you have slept through and neglected. If you will but wake now, rise now, meet God now, now at noon, God will call even this early. Have any of you slept through the whole day and come drowsily to your evening, to the closing of your eyes, to the end of your days? Yet rise now, and God shall call even this an early rising. If you can find a way to deceive your own souls and say, "We never heard God call us," if you neglected your former callings and forgot you have been called, yet is there one among you that denies God calls you now? But if you will wake now, and rise now, though this be late in your evening, in your age, yet God will call this early.

...meet God now.

The Fourth Sunday in Lent

Will you forgive that sin where I begun,
    Which is my sin, though it was done before?
Will you forgive those sins through which I run
    And do run still, though still I do deplore?
        When you have done, you have not done,
        For I have more.

Will you forgive that sin by which I've won
    Others to sin and made my sin their door?
Will you forgive that sin which I did shun
    A year or two, but wallowed in a score?
        When you have done, you have not done,
        For I have more.

I have a sin of fear, that when I've spun
    My last thread, I shall perish on the shore;
Swear by yourself that at my death your son
    Shall shine as he shines now and did before;
        And having done that, you have done,
        I have no more.

Prayer

O eternal and most gracious God,
you have held back your treasure of perfect joy and perfect glory
to be given by your own hand,
when we shall see you as you are and know you as we are known,
when we shall possess in an instant and possess forever
all that can lead to our happiness;
here in this world you give us such a foretaste of that joy
as to enable us to understand that treasure;
even small things come from you;
Nature reaches out her hand and gives us corn and wine and oil and milk,
but you fill her hand so that she may rain down her showers upon us;
Industry reaches out her hand to us
and gives us the fruit of our labor for ourselves and our posterity;
but your hand guides that hand when it sows and when it waters
and the increase is from you.
Friends reach out their hands to help us
but your hand supports the hand that supports us;
Humbly I pray you that you will continue your goodness
to the whole world and to this country and this church,
so that your Son when he comes in the clouds
may find us ready to give an account and able to stand in that judgment
for our faithful stewardship of your talents so abundantly committed to us;
Grant that time may be swallowed up in eternity
and hope swallowed in possession,
and all those called to your salvation
become one entire and everlasting sacrifice to you,
where you may receive delight from them
and they glory from you forevermore. Amen.

Reconciliation

Go and learn what this means, "I desire mercy, not sacrifice." For I have come to call not the righteous but sinners."

—St. Matthew 9:13

Reconciliation is a renewing of a former friendship that has been interrupted and broken. So this implies a present enmity and hostility with God and a former friendship with God and also a possibility of returning to that former friendship. Stop a little on each of these.

Shall we, between whom and nothing there was only a word, "Let us make human beings," we who are infinitely less than a mathematical point, than an imaginary atom, shall we human beings, this yesterday's nothing, this tomorrow's worse than nothing, be capable of that honor, that dishonorable honor, to be the enemy of God, that God who is more than can be imagined by us infinitely many times over. Human beings cannot be allowed so high a sin as enmity with God. The devil is only a slave to God and shall we be called God's enemy?

A reconciliation is required. There was a time when we were friends with God. God did not hate us from all eternity; God forbid. God had no purpose to fall out with us, for then God could never have admitted us to a friendship. No one can love another as a friend this year and mean to be their enemy next. God's foreknowledge that we should fall out was not a foreknowledge of anything that God meant to do, but only that we would become incapable of the continuation of this friendship. God therefore having made us in a state of love and friendship and not having done anything toward the violation of this friendship, continues in everlasting goodness toward us still, inviting us to accept the means of reconciliation and a return to the same state of friendship which we had at first.

You see what you had and how you lost it. If it might not be recovered, God would not call you to it. Be reconciled then to God. Embrace this reconciliation and this reconciliation shall restore you to that station that Adam had in Paradise. What would a soul give to be in that state of innocence that it had in baptism? Be reconciled to God and you have that, and an older innocence than that: the innocence of Paradise.

Go home, and if you find a burden of children, negligence in servants, crosses in your trading, narrowness and need in your estate, yet this need and this encumbered house shall be your Paradise. Go forth into the country, and if you find unseasonable weather, disease in your sheep and in your cattle, worms in your corn, backwardness in your rents, oppression in your landlord, yet this field of thorns and brambles shall be your Paradise. Lock yourself up in yourself, and though you find every room covered with the soot of former sins and shaken by the devil, yet this prison, this rack, this hell in your own conscience shall be your Paradise. And as in Paradise Adam at first needed no Savior, so when by this reconciliation in entertaining your Savior you are restored to this Paradise, you shall need no sub-Savior, no joint Savior, no other angel, no other saint. The holy one of Israel, who has wrought this reconciliation for you and brought it to you, shall establish it in you. We shall have a Sabbath here in the rest and peace of conscience and a life of one everlasting Sabbath hereafter, where to our rest there shall be added joy, and to our joy, glory, and this rest and joy and glory superinvested with that eternity which crowns them all.

Be reconciled to God.

Plenteous Redemption

Even in his servants he puts no trust, and his angels he charges with error.
—Job 4:18

Since with the Lord there is "plenteous redemption" (Psalm 130:7, KJV), that overflowing mercy of our God, those super-superlative merits of our Savior, that plenteous redemption may hold even in our likeness to the angels. For though great numbers of angels fell, yet greater numbers stood. For the gate is narrow and the road is hard that leads to life (St. Matthew 7:14), yet the room is spacious enough within. Why then by this plenteous redemption may we not hope that many more shall enter there than are excluded?

Apply to yourself that which Saint Cyril says of the angels, "Does it grieve you that any are fallen? Let this comfort you, that more stood than fell." If a suspicion that few shall be saved makes you afraid, look on this overflowing mercy of your God, this plenteous redemption, and you may find a well-grounded hope that there will be more with you than with those who perish. Live in such a warfare with temptations, in such a suspicion of your ordinary, indeed, of your best actions, as though there were one only to be saved and you would be that one. But live and die in such a sense of this plenteous redemption of your God as though neither you nor any other could lose salvation except by doubting of it. I do not doubt my own salvation and of whom can I have so much reason to doubt as of myself? When I come to heaven, shall I be able to say to any there, "Lord! How did you get here?" Was anyone less likely to come there than I?

There is not only one angel, a Gabriel, in heaven but "to you all angels cry aloud." Cherubim and seraphim are plural terms: many cherubs, many seraphs in heaven. There is not only one prince of the Apostles, a Peter, but "the glorious company of the Apostles praise you." There is not only a first martyr, a Stephen, but "the noble army of martyrs praise you." Whoever among our ancestors thought of any other way to China than by the Cape of Good Hope? Yet another way opened itself to Magellan. And who knows whether there may not yet be found a northeast and a northwest way there besides?

Go then to heaven in a humble thankfulness to God and holy cheerfulness in that way that God has shown to you. Do not announce too bitterly, too desperately, that everyone else is in error who does not think just as you think or who goes in a way that is not your way. God found folly, weakness, in the angels, yet more stood than fell. God finds weakness, wickedness, in us, yet Christ came to call not the righteous but sinners to repentance. And who, coming in that capacity, a repentant sinner, can be shut out or denied a part in this resurrection?

What repentant sinner can be denied?

He Came to Save

Then we who are alive, who are left, will be caught up in the clouds together
with them to meet the Lord in the air; and so we will be with the Lord forever.
—1 Thessalonians 4:17

It is a wonderful comfort to us that our blessed Savior mingles his realms, that he makes the realm of grace and the realm of glory all one, the Church and heaven all one. He assures us that if we see him here in his realm of grace, we have already begun to see him there in his realm of glory. If we see him as he looks in his Word and sacraments, in his realm of grace, we have begun to see him as he is in his essence, in the realm of glory. And when we pray, "Thy kingdom come," and mean only the realm of grace, he gives us more than we ask, a first understanding of the realm of glory in this life. This is his inexpressible mercy: that he mingles his realms and, where he gives us one, gives both.

So there is also a bright beam of comfort shown us in this text: that the number reserved for that realm is no small number. For although the psalm says, "The Lord looked down from heaven and saw no one that did good, no not one," and although Christ said, "When the Son of man comes, will he find faith on the earth?" we have, I say, a blessed beam of comfort shining out of this text, that it is no small number that is reserved for the realm. For the Apostle speaks not as of a few. Christ's preaching of the narrowness of the way and the straitness of the gate was not intended to make anyone imagine it to be impossible to enter but to be more industrious in seeking it. As he sent workers in plenty (abundant preaching), so he shall return a glorious harvest, a glorious addition to his realm.

He came to save. He did not come simply to offer salvation to those he intended to save, but he came really and truly to save. It was not to show a land of promise and then say, "There it is, but you shall never enter it." It was not to show us salvation and then say, "There it is, in baptism, in preaching, in the other sacrament, but wait, there is a decree of predestination against you and you shall have none of it." He came to save. And whom? Sinners. Those who, the more they admit that they are sinners, the nearer they are to this salvation.

He came to save.

God's Mercy Has No Season

Therefore the Lord himself will give you a sign. Look, the young woman is with child and shall bear a son, and shall name him Immanuel.

—Isaiah 7:14

We begin with that which is older than our beginning and shall outlive our end: the mercy of God. When we center our meditation on the mercy of God, even God's judgments cannot put us out of tune; we shall sing and be cheerful even in them. As God made grass for beasts before beasts were made, and beasts for humans before we were made, so in the re-creating of humanity God begins with that which was necessary for that which follows: mercy before judgment. No, to say that mercy was first is to diminish mercy. The names of first or last detract from it, for first and last are only rags of time, and God's mercy has no relationship to time, no limitation in time; it is not first or last but eternal, everlasting.

Let the devil make me so desperate as to imagine a time when there was no mercy and the devil has made me an atheist, to imagine a time when there was no God. If I take God's mercy away even one minute and say, "Now God has no mercy," for that minute I discontinue God's very being. As long as there has been love (and "God is love") there has been mercy. Mercy considered externally, in the practice and the effect, did not begin at the time when we were fallen and miserable but at our creation when we were nothing. So then we do not consider mercy as it is in God, an essential attribute, but as it is in us, an action, a working on us, and God takes all occasions to exercise that action and to shed that mercy on us.

The air is not so full of dust or atoms as the Church is of mercy, and as we can draw in no air without taking in that dust, those atoms, so here in the congregation we cannot draw in a word from the preacher, we cannot speak, we cannot sigh a prayer to God, except that whole breath and air is made of mercy.

If I should ask on what occasion God chose me and wrote my name in the Book of Life, I can more easily fear that it is not so than find a reason why it should be. God made sun and moon to distinguish seasons and day and night, and we can have the fruits of the earth only in their seasons. But there is no decree to separate the seasons of God's mercies. In Paradise the fruits were ripe the first minute, and in heaven it is always autumn. God's mercies are always in their maturity. We ask our daily bread, and God never says you should have come yesterday. God never says you must come again tomorrow, but if "today you would listen to his voice" (Psalm 95:7), today God will hear you.

If some ruler of the earth has so large a dominion in North and South that there is winter and summer together in that empire, or so large an extent East and West that there is day and night together, much more does God have mercy and judgment together. God brought light out of darkness, not out of a lesser light. God can bring your summer out of winter even if you have no spring. Even if in fortune or understanding or conscience you have been benighted till now, withered and frozen, clouded and eclipsed, damped and benumbed, smothered and stupefied till now, now God comes to you. God comes not as in the dawning of the day, not as in the bud of the spring, but as the sun at noon to light all shadows, as the sheaves in harvest to fill all need. All locations invite God's mercies and all times are God's seasons.

✳ ✳ ✳

...all times are God's seasons.

Holy Joy

For you have been my help, and in the shadow of your wings I sing for joy.
—Psalm 63:7

I would always raise and expand your hearts to a holy joy, to a joy in the Holy Spirit. There may be a justified fear that we do not always grieve enough for our sins. But there may be a justified fear also that we may fall into too great griefs and doubts of God's mercy, for God has accompanied and complicated almost all our bodily diseases with an extraordinary sadness, a predominant melancholy, a faintness of heart, a cheerlessness, a joylessness of spirit. And therefore I return often to this attempt to raise your hearts, to expand your hearts with a holy joy, joy in the Holy Spirit, for "in the shadow of God's wings" you may, you should, "sing for joy."

If you look at the world on a map, you find two hemispheres, two half-worlds. If you crush heaven into a map, you may find two hemispheres too, two half-heavens; half will be joy and half will be glory. In these two, the joy of heaven and the glory of heaven, all heaven is represented to us. And just as with the two-half hemispheres of the world, the first has been long known, but the other (that of America, which is richer in treasure) God reserved for later discovery, so even though God reserves that hemisphere of heaven which is its glory until the resurrection, still the other hemisphere, the joy of heaven, God opens to our discovery and delivers for our residence even while we live in this world.

Even if our natural life is no life but only a continual dying, still we have two lives besides that: an eternal life reserved for heaven, but still a heavenly life also, a spiritual life, even in this world. What Christ will say to your soul at the last judgment, "Enter into your Master's joy," he says to your conscience now, "Enter into your Master's joy." The everlastingness of the joy is the blessedness of the next life, but the entering comes here. For what Christ shall say then to us, "Come ye blessed," are words intended for those who are coming, who are on the way, though not yet home. Here in this world he bids us "Come"; there in the next he shall bid us "Welcome."

The angels of heaven have joy in your conversion, and can you be without that joy in yourself? The soul that is carefully presented to God, in a sincere confession, washed in the tears of contrition, embalmed in the blood of reconciliation, the blood of Jesus Christ, can assign no reason, can give no valid answer to that question: "Why are you cast down, O my soul, and why are you disquieted within me?" No one is so little that they can be lost under these wings; no one is so great that these wings cannot reach them.

✳ ✳ ✳

...you should "sing for joy."

"Rejoice" Is a Command

Rejoice always.
—1 Thessalonians 5:16

Our text lays a command on us: It is not, "You shall rejoice," by way of promise, but it is "Rejoice," see that you do rejoice, by way of command. We do not pass from the miseries of this life to the joys of heaven, but by joy in this life too. Those who feel no joy here shall find none hereafter. And when we pass from the first word, Rejoice, to the other, Rejoice always, we shall divide that into two sections: Rejoice in your prosperity, and Rejoice in your adversity too. But because it is "always," it must be in the one who is always, yesterday and today and the same forever: Joy in God, Joy in the Holy Spirit. There is a preparation and incomplete participation and possession of that joy in this life, but the fulfillment is reserved for our entrance into the Creator's joy: not only the joy given, which is here, but the joy that God is, which is there.

What is Joy? Just as rest is the end of motion (everything moves in order to rest), so Joy is the end of our desires (whatever we place our desires and affections on, it is so that we may enjoy it). Proverbs says, "When justice is done, it is a joy to the righteous" (21:15), to lie still and do no wrong is not joy. Joy is not that sort of rest, but like that of the sun which "like a strong man runs its course with joy" (Psalm 19:5). So this joy is the rest and testimony of a good conscience, that we have done those things we were called to do.

If those in ministry, whose function is to conduct services of worship, delight themselves by gathering riches; if a soldier delights himself in giving rules of agriculture or architecture; if a government official who should assist with counsel in times of crisis, delights in writing books of good counsel for posterity, none of this produces this joy, because though there may be motion and though there may be rest, it is not rest after the appropriate motion. Someone who has been wandering all day may be glad to find a good inn at night, but it is not truly joy because they are no nearer home. Joy is peace for having done what we ought to have done, and therefore the best evidence that we are at peace and in favor with God is that we can rejoice.

To test whether I am able by argument to prove all that I believe is the soul's university, where some are graduates and some are not. To test whether I am able to endure martyrdom for my beliefs, this is the rack and torture of the soul, and some are able to hold out and many are not. But to test whether I can rejoice in the peace which I have with God, this is the examination of the soul and every one must be examined, for it is a command: Rejoice always.

Rejoice always.

The Fifth Sunday in Lent

You have made me, and shall your work decay?
Repair me now; my end comes on in haste;
I run to death and death meets me as fast
And all my pleasures are like yesterday;
I dare not move my dim eyes any way;
Despair behind and death before both cast
Such terror, and my feeble flesh laid waste
By sin in it sinks down beneath hell's sway.
Yet you are still above and when I see
Your face turned toward me, then I rise again.
But our old subtle foe still tempting me
I cannot for one hour myself sustain;
Your grace may wing me against Satan's art
And you, like adamant, draw my iron heart.

Prayer

I lie in a grave of sin, O my God,
and where Lazarus had been for four days,
I have been for many years.
Why do you not call me, as you called him, "with a loud voice"
since my soul is as dead as his body was?
When your Son came to do the work of redemption,
you spoke, and those who heard it took it for thunder;
Your voice is a mighty voice:
mighty in power, so it may be heard,
mighty in obligation, so it should be heard,
mighty in operation, so it will be heard;
It is such a voice that your Son says,
"The dead shall hear it," and that is my state.
And why, O God, do you not speak to me
in that effective loudness?
Speak louder, O my God,
so that though I do hear you now,
then I may hear nothing but you.
I need your thunder, O my God,
your music will not serve me.
You speak loudest when you speak to the heart.

Fullness of Joy

Rejoice always.
—1 Thessalonians 5:16

It is not the function but the essence of God to do good, and when God does that, God is said to rejoice: "The Lord your God will make you very plenteous; and will rejoice over you for good"(Deuteronomy 30:9). Angels also; their role is to minister to us and when they see good results from their ministry, as when a sinner is converted, "There is joy in the presence of the angels of God"(St. Luke15:10). Christ himself had a ministry and when that was done, "Jesus rejoiced in the Holy Spirit" (St. Luke 10:21). To have something to do, to do it, and then to rejoice in having done it; to embrace a calling, to perform the duties of that calling, to joy and rest in the peaceful testimony of having done so, this is Christianly done, Christ did it; it is angelically done, angels do it; Godly done, God does it. The example as well as the rule repeats it to you: Rejoice always.

Not to feel joy is an argument against religious feeling; not to show that joy is evidence against thankfulness of the heart; and that is a stupidity, a contempt. If it is inside, it must be outside too. Unless I hear you say in your actions, I do rejoice, I cannot know that you have heard the Apostle say, Rejoice.

It is time to end; but as long as the hourglass has a gasp, as long as I have one, I would breathe in this air, this perfume, this breath of heaven, the contemplation of this joy. "Happy are the people" says the psalm, "who know the festal shout" (89:15). For although we are bound to rejoice always, it is not a blessed joy if we do not know upon what it is grounded, or if it is not grounded on everlasting blessedness. Joy in this life, where grief is mingled with joy, is called meat by Saint Bernard, and Christ calls his friends to eat. Joy in the next life, where it passes down without difficulty, without any opposition, is called drink; Christ calls his friends to drink. But the overflowing, the inebriation of the soul, is reserved for the last time, when our bodies as well as our souls shall enter into the participation of it: when we shall love everyone, as well as ourselves, and so have that joy of our own salvation multiplied by that number. We shall have that joy so many times over as there are souls saved because we will love them as ourselves. How infinitely shall this joy be enlarged in loving God, so far above ourselves, and all of them.

We have only this to add. Heaven is called by many precious names: life, simply and absolutely there is no life but that; kingdom, simply, absolutely there is no kingdom that is not subordinate to that; and Sabbath of Sabbaths, a Sabbath flowing into a Sabbath, a perpetual Sabbath; but the name that should enamor us most is that it is fullness of joy: fullness that needs no addition, fullness that allows no loss. And then, though in theology we place blessedness in the vision of God, yet the first thing that this sight of God shall produce in us is joy. The measure of our seeing of God is the measure of joy. See God here in God's blessings, and you shall see joy in those blessings there; and when you come to see the essence of God, then you shall have joy in this essence and in fullness—of which, may God give us such a foretaste here as may bind us to that inheritance hereafter which God's Son our Savior Christ Jesus has purchased for us with the inestimable price of his incorruptible blood. Amen.

We shall have that joy…

Praise and Prayer

Satisfy us in the morning with your steadfast love,
so that we may rejoice and be glad all our days.
—Psalm 90:14

Prayer and praise are the same thing. That prayer which our Savior gave us consists of seven petitions, and seven is a symbol of infinity. So, by beginning with glory and acknowledgment of his reigning in heaven and then ending in the same manner with acclamations of power and glory, it is made a circle of praise, and a circle is infinite too. The prayer and the praise are equally infinite. Infinitely poor and needy human beings who always have infinite things to pray for; infinitely rich and abundant human beings who always have infinite blessings to praise God for.

God's house in this world is called the house of prayer, but in heaven it is the house of praise. We will not be surprised with any new needs there, but one even incessant and everlasting tenor of thanksgiving. And it is a blessed beginning of that state now, to be continually involved in the commemoration of God's former goodness toward us. "O Lord, in the morning you hear my voice," says the psalm (5:3). What voice? The voice of prayer. But the psalmist's devotion did not begin when that prayer began; one part was before morning. "At midnight I rise to praise you," says another psalm (119:62). No doubt when the psalmist lay down, the account with God was settled. And then the first thing the psalmist does on waking again is not to beg God for more, but to bless God for former blessings. And as praise began all, so it passes through all. The psalmist extends it through all times, and all places, and would like to extend it through all persons, too, as we see by that expression which is so frequent in the psalms: "Let them thank the Lord for his steadfast love, for his wonderful works to humankind" (107:8).

If we compare these two incomparable duties, prayer and praise, it will be like this: our prayers besiege God, but our praises describe God. By prayer we incline and bend God; by praise we bind God with thanks for former benefits. Prayer is our petition, but praise is our evidence. In that we beg, in this we plead. God is not subject to any law, but yet God proceeds by precedent, and whenever we present thanksgiving for what God has done before, God does the same and more again. Prayer consists as much of praise for the past as of supplication for the future.

The saints in heaven are full, as full as they can hold, and yet they pray. Though they lack nothing, they pray that God would pour down on us graces necessary for our journey here as God has done on them in their station there. We are full, full of the gospel, present peace and plenty in the preaching thereof. We are full, and yet we pray. We pray that God would continue the gospel where it is, restore the gospel where it was, and transfer the gospel where it has not yet been preached.

✳ ✳ ✳

Prayer is praise.

Difficulties in Prayer

Martha said to Jesus, "Lord, if you had been here, my brother would not have died."

—St. John 11:21

I throw myself down in my room and I call in and invite God and God's angels there, and when they are there I neglect God and the angels for the noise of a fly, for the rattling of a coach, for the whining of a door. I talk on in the same posture of praying, eyes lifted up, knees bowed down, as though I prayed to God, and if God or the angels should ask me when I thought last of God in that prayer, I cannot tell. Sometimes I find that I had forgotten what I was about, but when I began to forget it, I cannot tell. A memory of yesterday's pleasures, a fear of tomorrow's dangers, a straw under my knee, a noise in my ear, a light in my eye, an anything, a nothing, a fancy, a chimera in my brain troubles me in my prayer. So certainly is there nothing, nothing in spiritual things, perfect in this world.

We may pray in the street, in the fields, in a fair; but it is a more acceptable and effectual prayer when we shut our doors and observe our fixed hours for private prayer in our room, and better when we pray on our knees than in our beds. But the greatest power of all is in the public prayer of the congregation.

If you pray for deliverance and are not delivered, do not think that you are not heard. Do not limit God in ways or times. But if you would be heard by God, hear God. If you would have God grant your prayers, do God's will. We pray you in Christ's stead that you would be reconciled to God; and are you reconciled? Do you dare hear the last trumpet now? Christ Jesus prays for you now to his Father in heaven that you might be converted; and are you converted? If the prayers of the Church militant and the Church triumphant and the head of churches, Christ Jesus, are not heard effectively on your behalf, yet they shall be in God's time. God's eternal choice shall infallibly work upon you.

So if your own prayers for your deliverance in any temporal or spiritual affliction are not heard at present, persevere for yourselves as the churches and the head of them persevere in your behalf, and God will certainly deliver you and strengthen you to fight out God's battle all the way.

✳ ✳ ✳

Persevere in prayer.

Pray Specifically; Pray Frequently

Martha said to Jesus, "Lord, if you had been here, my brother would not have died."

—St. John 11:21

I must not wrap up all my needs in general terms in my prayers but descend to particulars, for this places my devotion on particular considerations of God: to consider every attribute of God, what God has done for me in power, what in wisdom, what in mercy. And this is a great assistance in establishing and deepening devotion.

It is a kind of unthankfulness to thank God too generally and not to delight in insisting on the weight and measure and proportion and goodness of every particular mercy. It is also an irreverent and inconsiderate thing not to take my particular wants into my thoughts and into my prayers so that I may acquire a holy knowledge that I have nothing, nothing except from God and by prayer. And as God is an accessible God, and ever open to receive your petitions no matter how small the matter, so God is an inexhaustible God who can give infinitely and a tireless God who cannot be pressed too much. Therefore, Christ has given us a parable of getting bread at midnight by importunity and not otherwise, and another parable of a judge who heard the widow's cause by importunity and not otherwise. We have also the story of the woman of Canaan who overcame him on behalf of her daughter by importunity when except by importunity she could not get so much as an answer, a denial at his hands.

Pray personally. Do not rely on dead or living saints. Your mother the Church prays for you, but pray for yourself too. She can open her bosom and put the breast to your mouth, but you must draw and suck for yourself. Pray personally and pray frequently. Pray frequently and pray fervently. God did not take offense at being awakened by the psalmist and called up, as if God were asleep at our prayers, and to be called upon, as though God were slack in relieving our needs. It is not enough to pray or to confess in general terms. It is not enough to have prayed once. Christ does not only excuse but command importunity.

Little do you know what you have received at God's hands, by the prayers of the saints in heaven who wrap you in their general prayers for the church on earth. Little do you know what the public prayers of the congregation, what the private prayers of particular devout friends who lament your carelessness and negligence in prayer for yourself, have wrung and extorted out of God's hands in their charitable importunity for you. And therefore, at last, make yourself fit to do for others that which others have done for you in assisting you with their prayers. Will you not save the life of another who asks you when perhaps your soul has been saved by another who prayed for you?

Pray frequently; pray fervently.

God Comes to the Church

And blessed is anyone who takes no offense at me.
                                    —St. Matthew 11:6

Saint Augustine said, "Lord, you have made us for yourself and our hearts cannot rest until they get to you." But can we come to God here? We cannot. Where then is our preparation, our initiation, our beginning of blessedness? Beloved, though we cannot come to God here, here God comes to us. Here, in the prayers of the congregation, God comes to us. Here, in this ordinance of preaching, God comes to us. Here, in the administration of the sacrament, God seals, ratifies, confirms all to us. And to rest in these seals and means of reconciliation to God, we ought not to be scandalized, not offended. We ought not to be offended in God or question these means which God has ordained. This is our preparation, our initiation, and the beginning of blessedness beyond which nothing can be offered in this life.

The needle of a compass, though it may shake a long while, yet will rest at last, and though it does not look directly, exactly toward the North Pole, but will have some variation, yet, for all that variation, it will rest. So, though your heart may have some variations, some deviations, some aspirations from that direct point toward which it should be aimed, an absolute conformity of your will to the will of God, yet, though you lack something of that, give your soul rest. Settle your soul in such a security as this earthly condition can permit and believe that God receives as much glory in your repentance as in your innocence, and that the mercy of God in Christ is as good a pillow to rest your soul on after a sin as the grace of God in Christ is a shield and protection for your soul before.

In a word, this is our preparation, our initiation, and the beginning of blessedness beyond which there can be no blessedness offered here. It is first to be satisfied that there are certain and constant means ordained by Christ for our reconciliation to God in all cases in which a Christian soul can be distressed and that such a treasure is deposited in the Church. And then, it is to have the testimony of a good conscience, that you have sincerely applied those general helps to your particular soul. Come this far, and then, as the suburbs touch the city, and the porch touches the church and delivers you into it, so shall this preparation, this initiation, and this beginning of blessedness deliver you over to the everlasting blessedness of heaven.

...treasure in the Church.

The Catholic Church

And when he comes, he will prove the world wrong about sin and righteousness and judgment.

—St. John 16:8

The Church loves the name of Catholic, and it is a glorious and harmonious name. Love those things in which it is Catholic and in which it is harmonious, those universal and fundamental doctrines which in all Christian ages and in all Christian churches have been agreed by all to be necessary to salvation, and then you are a true Catholic.

Let no one say, "I can have all this at God's hands immediately and never trouble the church; I can have my pardon from God without all these formalities, by secret repentance." It is true, beloved, a true repentance is never frustrated. But yet, if you think of yourself as a little church, a church to yourself, because you have heard it said that you are a little world, a world in yourself, that figurative representation shall not save you. Though you may be a world to yourself, yet if you have no more corn or oil or milk than grows in yourself or flows from yourself, you will starve. Though you be a church in your imagination, if you have no more seals of grace, no more absolution of sin, than you can give yourself, you will perish. However God may take your own word at home, yet God accepts the church on your behalf as better security. Join, therefore, always with the communion of saints.

While you are a member of that congregation that speaks to God with a thousand tongues, believe that you speak, too, with all those tongues. And though you know your own prayers unworthy to come up to God because you lift an eye which is only just withdrawn from a licentious glance, and hands which are guilty still of unrepented uncleanness, a tongue that has recently blasphemed, a heart which even now breaks the walls of this House of God and steps home or runs abroad in the memory or the plotting of new pleasures or profits, and though this makes you think your own prayers ineffectual, yet believe that some more honest person than yourself stands by you and that when they pray with you, they pray for you. And believe that if there is one righteous individual in the congregation, you are made more acceptable to God by that one's prayers. Let the Holy Spirit convince you and assure you of an orderly church established for your relief and that the application of yourself to this judgment, the church, shall enable you to stand upright in that other judgment, the last judgment.

Never say, there is no church without error, therefore I will be bound by none but shape a church of my own or be a church to myself. What greater injustice then to propose no image, no pattern to yourself to imitate and yet propose yourself for a pattern, for an image to be worshiped? You will have singular opinions and singular ways differing from all others, and all that are not of your opinion must be heretics, and all reprobates that go not your way. Adopt good patterns for yourself and thereby become a fit pattern for others.

Join with the saints.

Palm Sunday

The Cross

Since Christ embraced the Cross itself, dare I
His image, the image of his Cross deny?
Would I have profit by the sacrifice
And dare the chosen Altar to despise?
It bore all other sins, but is it fit
That it should bear the sin of scorning it?
From me, no pulpit, no misguided law,
Nor scandal taken shall this Cross withdraw,
It shall not, for it cannot; for the loss
Of this Cross would become another Cross.
Who can deny me power and liberty
To stretch my arms and my own Cross to be?
Swim, and at every stroke you are your Cross;
The yard and mast make one where deep seas toss;
Look down and see the Crosses in small things;
Look up and see birds raised on their crossed wings;
All the globe's frame and spheres are nothing else
But the meridians crossing parallels.
Be covetous of Crosses, let none fall;
Cross no one else, but cross yourself in all.
Then will the Cross of Christ work fruitfully
Within our hearts when we love harmlessly
That Cross's pictures much, and with more care
That Cross's children, which our Crosses are.

Prayer

O most glorious and most gracious God,
into whose presence our own consciences make us afraid to come
and from whose presence we cannot hide ourselves,
hide us in the wounds of your Son our Savior Jesus Christ;
We renounce, O Lord, all our confidence in this world,
for this world passes away and all the desires thereof.
We renounce all our confidence in our own merits,
for we remain unprofitable servants to you.
We renounce all confidence even in our own confessions,
for our sins are above number if we could reckon them,
and past finding out if we could find them
in all those dark corners where we have multiplied them;
Yes, we renounce all confidence even in our own repentance,
for we have found by many lamentable experiences
that we never perform our promises to you,
never perfect our purposes in ourselves,
but relapse again and again into those sins of which we have repented;
We have no confidence in this world
but in the One who has taken possession of the next world for us
by sitting down at your right hand;
We have no confidence in our own repentance,
but in that Blessed Spirit who is the author of them
and loves to perfect her own works and build upon her
        own foundations, we have.
Accept them therefore, O Lord, for your Blessed Spirit's sake
who is in us now
and must be whenever we pray acceptably.

To Fall from God's Hands

The one who believes and is baptized will be saved; but the one who does not believe will be condemned.

—St. Mark 16:16

"It is a fearful thing," says the Apostle, "to fall into the hands of the living God" (Hebrews 10:31). But to fall out of the hands of the living God is a horror beyond our expression, beyond our imagination:

That God should let my soul fall out of God's hand into a bottomless pit and roll an unremovable stone upon it and leave it to that which it finds there (and it shall find that there which it never imagined until it came there) and never think more of that soul, never have more to do with it;

That from that providence of God that studies the life and preservation of every weed and worm and ant and spider and toad and viper, there should never, never any beam flow out on me;

That that God who looked on me when I was nothing and called me out of the womb and depth of darkness, will not look on me now, when, though a miserable and a banished and a damned creature, yet I am God's creature still and contribute something to God's glory even in my damnation;

That that God who has often looked on me in my foulest uncleanness and when I had shut out the eye of the day, the sun, and the eye of the night, the taper, and the eyes of all the world with curtains and windows and doors, did yet see me and see me in mercy by making me see that God saw me should be so turned from me to the glorious saints and angels that no saint or angel or Christ Jesus himself should ever pray God to look toward me, never remember that such a soul exists;

That that God who has so often said to my soul, "Why will you die?" and so often sworn to my soul, "I would not have you die, but live," will neither let me die nor let me live, but die an everlasting life, and live an everlasting death;

That that God, who could not get into me by standing and knocking, by God's ordinary means of entering, by God's word, God's mercies, has applied judgment and has shaken the house, this body, with sickness and disease, and set this house on fire with fevers, and frightened the master of the house, my soul, with horrors and heavy fears, and so made an entrance into me;

That this God at last should let this soul go away like a smoke, like a vapor, like a bubble, and that then this soul cannot be a smoke, or a vapor, or a bubble, but must lie in darkness as long as the Lord of light is light itself, and never a spark of that light reach to my soul. What Tophet is not Paradise, what brimstone is not amber, what gnashing is not a comfort, what gnawing of the worm is not a tickling, what torment is not a marriage bed to this damnation, to be excluded eternally, eternally, eternally from the sight of God?

This damnation, which consists in the loss of the sight and presence of God, shall be heavier to us than others because God has so graciously and in so many ways appeared to us, in the pillar of fire, in the light of prosperity, and in the pillar of the cloud. But to those who believe aright and overcome all temptations to a wrong belief, God shall give the fullness of joy, and joy rooted in glory, and glory established in eternity, and this eternity is God. To those who believe and overcome, God shall give an everlasting presence and fulfillment. Amen.

✳ ✳ ✳

...to fall from God's hands.

The Certainty of Death

Who can live and never see death?
　　　　　—Psalm 89:48

Let no man, no woman, no devil offer the suggestion, "Perhaps we may die," much less a, "Surely we shall not die," unless they are provided with an answer to this question, unless they can give an example and produce the name and history of that one who has lived and not seen death. We are all conceived in close prison in our mother's womb; we are close prisoners all. When we are born, we are born only to the liberty of the house, prisoners still, though within larger walls; and then all our life is only a going out to the place of execution, to death.

Now was there anyone seen to sleep in the cart between Newgate and Tyborne? Between the prison and the place of execution, does anyone sleep? Yet we sleep all the way; from the womb to the grave we are never fully awake, but pass on with such dreams and imagination as these: I may live as well as another and why should I die rather than another? But awake and tell me, says this text, "Who is the one that you speak of? Who is it that lives and shall not see death?"

Then if we consider violent deaths, casual deaths, it is almost a scornful thing to see with what wantonness and sportfulness death plays with us. We have seen a man cannon-proof in the time of war, and slain with his own pistol in the time of peace. We have seen a man recovered after his drowning and live to hang himself. But that one kind of death which is general, we have learned to call "natural death," though, indeed, there is nothing more unnatural. Only the commonness makes it natural.

Take a flat map and here is east and there is west, as far apart as two points can be put. But reduce this flat map to roundness, which is the true form, and then east and west touch with one another and are all one. So consider our life rightly to be a circle: "You are dust, and to dust you shall return." In this, the circle, the two points meet; the womb and the grave are only one point, they make only one station, there is only a step from that to this. And so there was a custom in the early church that they called the martyrs' days on which they suffered their birth days; birth and death are all one. Their death was a birth to them into another life, into the glory of God. It ended one circle, and created another, for immortality and eternity is a circle: not a circle where two points meet but a circle made at once. This life is a circle made with a compass that passes from point to point; that life is a circle stamped with a print, an endless and perfect circle, as soon as it begins. Of this circle the mathematician is our great and good God. The other circle we make up ourselves; we bring the cradle and grave together by a course of nature. Everyone does.

...we are never fully awake.

Death Is Certain

The last enemy to be destroyed is death.
—1 Corinthians 15:26

"*Perhaps*," says Saint Augustine, "is a word of accident, of chance occurrence. There is room for that word in all human actions except death." Augustine gives this example: two people are married; shall they have children? Perhaps, says Augustine, they are young; perhaps they shall. And shall those children live to be adults? Perhaps; they are from healthy parents, perhaps they shall. And when they have lived to be adults, shall they be good people? Perhaps, still; they are of good parents, it may be they shall. But when they are come to death, shall this good person die? Here, says Augustine, the "perhaps" vanishes. Here it is infallibly, inevitably, irrecoverably they must die.

Do we not die even in our birth? The breaking of prison is death, and what is our birth but a breaking of prison? As soon as we were clothed by God, our clothing was an emblem of death. In the skins of dead beasts, God covered the skins of dying humans. As soon as God set us to work, our very occupation was an emblem of death. Our work was to dig the ground; not to dig pitfalls for others, but graves for ourselves. Has anyone here forgotten today that yesterday is dead? The bell tolls for today and it will ring out soon and ring for every one of us in regard to this day. "We die every day," says Saint Jerome, "and we die all the day long," and because we are not absolutely dead, we call that an eternity, an eternity of dying. And is there comfort in that state? Why, that is the state of hell itself: eternal dying, and not dead.

Death comes equally to us all and makes us all equal when it comes. The ashes of an oak in the chimney are no epitaph of that oak, to tell me how high or how large it was. It does not tell me what flocks it sheltered while it stood nor whom it hurt when it fell. The dust of great persons' graves is speechless too; it says nothing, it distinguishes nothing. If the wind blows it toward you, the dust of a wretch you would not look at will trouble your eyes as much as the dust of a prince whom you could not look at. And when a whirlwind has blown the dust of the churchyard into the church and the sexton sweeps out the dust of the church into the churchyard, who will undertake to sift that dust again and to pronounce, this is the patrician, this is the noble flower, and this the yeoman, this the plebeian bran?

God calls the good to take them from their dangers and God takes the bad to take them from their triumph. And therefore do not complain that you go nor that worse people stay, for God can make profit of both. God reprieves some to mend them or to make others better by their work. How ever long you live, how ever long you lie sick, you die a sudden death if you never thought of it.

God did not make death, says Sappho, and therefore Saint Augustine makes a reasonable prayer to God: "Let not death, O Lord, which you did not make, have dominion over me whom you did make."

Let not death have dominion…

Make This Your Day

Our God is a God of salvation,
and to God, the Lord, belongs escape from death.
—Psalm 68:20

Take in the whole day, from the hour that Christ received the Passover on Thursday until the hour in which he died the next day. Make this present day that day in your devotions. Consider what he did and remember what you have done. Before he instituted and celebrated the sacrament, he proceeded to that act of humility to wash his disciples' feet, even Peter's, who for a while resisted him. In your preparation for the holy and blessed sacrament, have you with a sincere humility sought a reconciliation with the world, even with those who have been averse from it and refused that reconciliation with you? If so, and not otherwise, you have spent the first part of his last day in conformity with him.

After the sacrament he spent the time until night in prayer, in preaching, in psalms. Have you considered that a worthy receiving of the sacrament consists of a continuation of holiness afterwards as well as a preparation before? If so, you have in this also conformed yourself to him. So Christ spent his time until night: "At night he went into the garden to pray," and he spent much time in prayer. How much? Because it is said that he prayed there three separate times and that, returning to his disciples after his first prayer and finding them asleep, he asked, "Could you not watch with me one hour?" it is supposed that he spent three hours in prayer. I scarce dare ask you where you went or how you disposed of yourself when it grew dark and after last night. If that time were spent in a holy recommendation of yourself to God and a submission of your will to God's, it was spent in conformity to him. In that time and in those prayers was his agony and bloody sweat. I will hope that you did pray, but not every ordinary and customary prayer. Prayer actually accompanied by shedding of tears and disposed in a readiness to shed blood for his glory puts you into conformity with him.

About midnight, he was taken and bound with a kiss. Are you not too conformed to him in that? Is that not too literally, too exactly, your case: at midnight to have been taken and bound with a kiss? From there, he was carried back to Jerusalem, and examined and buffeted and delivered over to the custody of those officers from whom he received all those blows and violence, the covering of his face, the spitting upon his face, the blasphemies of words, and the stinging blows which the gospel mentions. In that time came the crowing of the cock which called Peter to his repentance. How you passed all that time last night, you know. If you did anything then that needed Peter's tears and have not shed them, let me be your cock: do it now. Now your Master looks back upon you: do it now.

* * *

Conform yourself to him...

Be Conformed to Christ

Our God is a God of salvation,
and to God, the Lord, belongs escape from death.
—Psalm 68:20

In the morning, as soon as it was day, the authorities held a counsel in the High Priest's hall. They agreed on their evidence against him and then carried him to Pilate, who was to be his judge. Did you accuse yourself when you awoke this morning, and were you content even with false accusations; that is, rather to suspect actions to be sin which were not than to smother and justify those that were truly sins? Then you spent that hour in conformity with him. Pilate found no evidence against him, and therefore to ease himself and to compliment Herod, Pilate sent him to Herod. Herod sent him back to Pilate to proceed against him, and this was about eight o'clock.

Have you been content to come to this examination of your conscience, to sift it, to follow it from the sins of your youth to your present sins, from the sins of your bed to the sins of your board, and from the substance to the circumstance of your sins? That's time spent like your Savior's. Pilate would have saved Christ by using the privilege of the day in his behalf because that day one prisoner was to be set free, but they chose Barabbas. He would have saved him from death by satisfying their fury and inflicting other torments on him: scourging and crowning with thorns and loading him with many scornful and shameful rebukes. But this did not save him; they demanded a crucifixion.

Have you gone about to redeem your sin by fasting, by alms, by disciplines and mortifications to satisfy the justice of God? That will not serve, that's not the right way. We press for an utter crucifying of that sin that governs you; and that conforms you to Christ. Toward noon, Pilate gave judgment and they made such haste to execution that by noon he was upon the cross. There now hangs that sacred body on the cross, rebaptized in his own tears and sweat and embalmed alive in his own blood. There is that heart of compassion, so conspicuous that you may see it through his wounds. There those glorious eyes are growing faint in their light so that the sun, ashamed to survive them, departs with its light as well. And then that Son of God delivers that soul (which was never out of his Father's hands) by a new way, a voluntary breathing of it out into his Father's hands.

So, as God breathed a soul into the first Adam, so this second Adam breathed his soul into God, into the hands of God. There we leave you in that blessed dependence, to hang upon him that hangs upon the cross; there bathe in his tears and lie down in peace in his grave until he grant you a resurrection and an ascension into the kingdom which he has purchased for you with his own priceless blood.

Hang upon him…

The Water of Baptism

The earth was a formless void and darkness covered the face of the deep, while a wind from God swept over the face of the waters.

—Genesis 1:2

The water of baptism is the water that runs through all the early teachers of the church. All of them who had occasion to dive or dip in these waters make these first waters in the creation the symbol of baptism. So Tertullian makes the water the voyage and the harbor, the circumference and the center of the Holy Spirit. And so Jerome calls these waters the mother of the world: The waters brought forth the whole world as a mother is delivered of the child. And this symbol of baptism, says John of Damascus, foreshows that the waters also should bring forth the Church, that the Church of God should be born through the sacrament of baptism. Saint Basil said that the Spirit of God worked upon the waters in the creation because the Spirit meant to do so afterwards in the regeneration of humanity. And therefore, until the Holy Spirit has moved upon our children in baptism let us not think that we have done everything for those children.

And for ourselves, in baptism we are sunk under water and then raised above the water again. Such was the manner of baptizing in the Christian Church, by immersion, and not by pouring until recent times. Augustine says our corrupt affections and our inordinate love of this world are that which must be drowned in us. A love of peace and holy assurance and acceptance of God's sacrament is what lifts us above the water.

The Spirit of God is motion, the Spirit of God is also rest. In the proper consideration of baptism a true Christian is both moved and settled, moved to awareness of the breaking of commitments, settled in the knowledge of the mercy of God, in the merits of Christ, with a Godly sorrow.

This is the motion and this is the rest of the Spirit of God on these waters. God brings us to a desire for baptism, and settles us in a sense of the obligation first and then of the benefits of baptism. We are allowed to go into the way of temptation (for every calling has particular temptations), and then we are settled by God's preceding or following grace. God moves in submitting us to tribulation and settles us in finding that our tribulations serve best of all to conform us to Christ Jesus. God moves in removing us by the hand of death and settles us in an assurance that it is God who now lets us depart in peace. And the one who lays our souls in that safe cabinet, the bosom of Abraham, keeps an eye on every grain and atom of our dust, wherever it may be blown, and keeps a room at God's right hand for that body when it is reunited in a blessed resurrection.

God is motion and rest.

Easter Day

At the round earth's imagined corners, blow
Your trumpets, angels, and arise, arise
From death, you numberless infinities
Of souls, and to your scattered bodies go,
All whom the flood did, and fire shall overthrow,
All whom war, dearth, age, sickness, tyrannies,
Despair, law, chance hath slain, and you whose eyes
Shall behold God and never taste death's woe.
But let them sleep, Lord, and me mourn a space,
For if, above all these, my sins abound
'Tis late to ask abundance of your grace
When we are there; here on this holy ground
Teach me how to repent, for that's as good
As if you'd sealed my pardon with your blood.

Prayer

Bring us, O Lord God, at our last awakening,
into the house of God and gate of heaven
that we may dwell in that place
where there is no cloud nor sun,
no darkness nor dazzling, but one equal light,
no noise nor silence, but one equal music,
no fears nor hopes, but one equal possession,
no foes nor friends, but one equal communion and identity,
no ends nor beginnings, but one equal eternity;
and keep us, Lord, so awake in the duties of our callings
that we may sleep in your peace and wake in your glory
to an unending possession of that realm
which your Son our Savior Jesus Christ
has purchased for us with the price of his own blood. Amen.

New Heavens

But, in accordance with his promise, we wait for new heavens and a new earth, where righteousness is at home.

—2 Peter 3:13

In the first discoveries of the unknown parts of the world, the maps made were very uncertain, very imperfect. So, in the discovery of these new heavens and this new earth, our maps will be imperfect. It is said of old mapmakers that when they had said all that they knew of a country, they said that the rest was possessed by giants or witches or spirits or wild beasts so that they could explore no further. So when we have traveled as far as we can with safety, that is as far as ancient or modern explorers lead us in the discovery of these new heavens and new earth, yet we must say at last that it is a country inhabited by angels and archangels, with cherubim and seraphim, and that we can look no further into it with these eyes.

Where it is, we do not ask. We rest in this: that it is the habitation prepared for the blessed saints of God.

In that heaven the moon is more glorious than our sun, and the sun as glorious as the one who made it. In this new earth all the waters are milk and all the milk is honey; all the grass is corn and all the corn is manna; all the clods of earth are gold and all the gold of countless carats; all the minutes are ages and all the ages eternity, everything is every minute in the highest exaltation, as good as it can be, and yet superexalted and infinitely multiplied by every minute's addition; every minute is infinitely better than ever it was before. Of these new heavens and this new earth we must say at last that we can say nothing. For human eye has not seen nor ear heard nor heart conceived the state of this place.

We limit our consideration with that horizon with which the Holy Spirit has limited us: that it is that new heaven and new earth where righteousness is at home.

✳ ✳ ✳

...a new heaven and a new earth.

Heaven All the Way

For you have been my help, and in the shadow of your wings I sing for joy.
—Psalm 63:7

The angels of heaven have joy in your conversion, and can you be without that joy in yourself? Howling is the noise of hell, singing is the voice of heaven; sadness is the depression of hell, rejoicing is the serenity of heaven. And those who do not have this joy here lack one of the best pieces of evidence for the joys of heaven, and have neglected or refused that proof which God uses to bind the bargain: that true joy in this world shall flow into the joy of heaven as a river flows into the sea.

This joy shall not be put out in death and a new joy kindled in me in heaven; but my soul, as soon as it is out of my body, will be in heaven. It will not wait for the possession of heaven or the perfection of the sight of God until it has ascended through air and fire and moon and sun and planets and firmament to that place which we imagine to be heaven, but without the thousandth part of a minute's stop it is immediately in a glorious light which is heaven—for all the way to heaven is heaven.

As those angels that come from heaven bring heaven with them and are in heaven here, so that soul that goes to heaven meets heaven here. And as those angels do not put off heaven by coming, so those souls put on heaven in their going. My soul shall not go toward heaven but go by heaven to heaven, to the heaven of heavens. And we go there, not because we are without joy and must have joy infused into us, but so that, as Christ says, "Our joy might be full," so that it may be perfected, sealed with an everlastingness.

As Christ promises that no one shall take our joy from us, so neither shall death itself take it away, nor so much as interrupt it or discontinue it. In the face of death when it lays hold upon me, and in the face of the devil when the devil attempts to take me, I shall see the face of God for everything shall be a mirror to reflect God upon me.

In the agonies of death, in the anguish of that dissolution, in the sorrows of that departure, I shall have a joy which shall no more evaporate than my soul shall evaporate; a joy that shall pass up and put on a more glorious garment above, and be joy superinvested in glory. Amen.

I shall see God...

What Is Blessedness?

And blessed is anyone who takes no offense at me.
— St. Matthew 11:6

I would ask permission of the angels of heaven, of the Holy Spirit also, to say a little of the everlasting blessedness of the realm of heaven. The tongues of angels cannot, the tongues of the Holy Spirit, the authors of the books of scripture, have not told us what this blessedness is. What then shall we say except this?

Blessedness itself is God. Our blessedness is our possession, our union with God. Of what does this consist? Many great teachers place this blessedness, this union with God, in this: that in heaven I shall see God, see God face to face. We do not see anyone in that way in this world. In this world we see only outsides; in heaven I shall see God, and God's essence.

But many other teachers place this blessedness, this union with God, in love: that in heaven I shall love God. Now love presumes knowledge, for we can only love what we understand or think we understand. There in heaven I shall know God, which means I shall be admitted not only to an adoration of God, a reverence of God, but to more familiarity with God, more equality with God, so that I may love God.

But even love itself, as noble a passion as it is, is only a pain unless we enjoy what we love. Therefore still other teachers place this blessedness, this union of our souls with God, in our joy, our enjoyment of God. In this world we enjoy nothing. Enjoyment requires continuance, and here all things are fluid and transitory. There I shall enjoy and possess forever God as God is.

But every one of these, to see God, or to love God, or to enjoy God, has seemed to some too narrow to include fully this blessedness beyond which nothing can be imagined. Therefore other teachers place this blessedness in all these together. And truly, if any of these did exclude any others so that I might see God and not love God or love God without enjoyment, it could not well be called blessedness; but those who have any one of these have every one and all.

In heaven, therefore, I shall have not only vision, not only a seeing, but a beholding, a contemplating of God. I shall have an uninterrupted sight of God. I shall look, and never look away; not look, and look again, as here, but look, and look still.

I shall see the whole light. Here I see some parts of the air enlightened by the sun, but I do not see the whole light of the sun. There I shall see God entirely, all God; I myself shall be all light to see that light by. Here I have one faculty enlightened and another left in darkness; my understanding sometimes clear, my will at the same time perverted. There I shall be all light, no shadow upon me; my soul invested in the light of joy and my body in the light of glory.

I shall be light...

We Shall Know

For it is the God who said, "Let light shine out of darkness," who has shone in our hearts to give the light of the knowledge of the glory of God in the face of Jesus Christ.

—2 Corinthians 4:6

In heaven, Christ said, we shall be as the angels (St. Matthew 22:30). The knowledge which I have by nature shall have no clouds; here it has. That which I have by grace shall have no reluctance, no resistance; here it has. That which I have by revelation shall have no suspicion, no jealousy; here it has. There our curiosity shall have this noble satisfaction, that we shall know how the angels know, by knowing as they know.

We shall not pass from author to author as in a grammar school, nor from art to art as in a university; but, as that general who knighted his whole army, God will create us all doctors in a minute. That great library, those infinite volumes of the Books of Creation, shall be taken away, quite away, no more nature; those revered manuscripts written with God's own hand, the scriptures themselves, shall be taken away, quite away, no more preaching, no more reading of scriptures; and that great school mistress, experience and observation, shall be removed, no new thing to be done, and in an instant I shall know more than they all could reveal to me. I shall know, not only as I know already, that a beehive, an anthill, is a small realm, that a flower which lives only a day is an abridgment of that ruler who lives out the three score and ten years. But I shall know also that all these ants and bees and flowers and rulers and realms, although they may serve as examples and comparisons to one another, yet they are all as nothing, altogether nothing, less than nothing, infinitely less than nothing, to that which shall then be the subject of my knowledge, for it is the knowledge of the glory of God.

Can you hope to pour the whole sea into a thimble or to take the whole world into your hand? And yet, that is easier than to comprehend the joy and the glory of heaven in this life. Nor is there anything that makes this more incomprehensible than the nature of eternity itself, that we shall be with God forever. For this eternity, this everlastingness is incomprehensible to us in this life.

How barren a thing is arithmetic, and yet arithmetic will tell you how many single grains of sand will fill this hollow vault to the sky. How empty a thing is rhetoric, and yet rhetoric will make absent and remote things present to your understanding. How weak a thing is poetry, and yet poetry is able to counterfeit the creation and make things that are not as though they were. How weak are all assistances if they are used to express this eternity! The best help I can give you is to use your own eternity well. Saint Gregory calls our whole course of life our eternity. He says it is only justice that those who have sinned during their own eternity, their own life span, should suffer out God's eternity. So, if you suffer out your own eternity in submitting yourself to God in the whole course of your life, in surrendering your will entirely to God and glorifying God in a constant patience in all your tribulation, it will be God's justice to repay trouble to those who trouble you and, to you who are troubled, that you shall be caught up in the clouds to meet the Lord in the air and so to be with the Lord forever.

...we shall know as the angels know.

We Shall See Him

For it is the God who said, "Let light shine out of darkness," who has shone in our hearts to give the light of the knowledge of the glory of God in the face of Jesus Christ.

—2 Corinthians 4:6

The glory of Christ is the glory of sitting down at the right hand of God in our flesh, in his human nature, the glory he had before the world, for he had it in the eternal decree. And that's the glory of God which we shall know, know by having it. We shall have a knowledge of the true glory, the essential glory of God, because we shall see God as God is. And I shall know as I am known. That glory shall expand us, enlarge us, give us an inexpressible capacity and then fill it. We shall never comprehend that glory, the essential glory, but that glory which Christ has received in his human nature we shall comprehend, we shall know, by having. We shall receive a crown of glory that does not fade. It is a crown that encompasses us so no danger can enter from any side, and a crown that does not fade, that fears no winter. We shall have interest in all we see, and we shall see the treasure of all knowledge, the face of Christ Jesus.

Then and there, we shall have an abundant satisfaction and accomplishment of all Saint Augustine's three wishes. He wished to have seen Rome in her glory, to have heard Saint Paul preach, and to have seen Christ in the flesh. We shall have all. We shall see such a Jerusalem that Rome, which is said to be the whole world, would be but a village to this Jerusalem. We shall hear Saint Paul with the whole choir of heaven pour himself out in that acclamation, "Salvation belongs to our God who is seated on the throne, and to the Lamb!" (Revelation 7:10).

And we shall see, and see forever, Christ in that flesh which has done enough for his friends and is safe enough from his enemies. We shall see him in a transfiguration, all clouds of sadness removed, all his tears changed to pearls, all his blood drops into rubies, all the thorns of his crown into diamonds. For where we shall see the walls of his palace to be sapphire and emerald and amethyst and all stones that are precious, what shall we not see in the face of Christ Jesus? And whatever we do see, by that very sight becomes ours.

We shall see the face of Christ.

Look Him in the Face

For it is the God who said, "Let light shine out of darkness," who has shone in our hearts to give the light of the knowledge of the glory of God in the face of Jesus Christ.

—2 Corinthians 4:6

Do not, therefore, be strangers to this face. See him here, that you may know him and he you there. See him in the preaching of his word. See him in the sacrament.

Look him in the face as he lay in the manger, poor, and then do not murmur at temporal wants, and doubt not that God has large and strange ways to supply you.

Look him in the face in the temple, disputing there at twelve years, and then apply yourself to God, to the contemplation of God, to meditation on God, to a conversation with God.

Look him in the face in his father's house, a carpenter and only a carpenter; take a calling and contain yourself in that calling. But bring him nearer and look him in the face as he looked on Good Friday, when he whose face the angels desire to look on, he who was fairer than the children of humans, as the prophet says, was so marred, more than anyone, as another prophet says, that they hid their faces from him and despised him, when he who bore up the heavens bowed down his head, and he who gives breath to all gave up the ghost.

And then look him in the face again as he looked on Easter day, not lamed upon the cross, not decayed in the grave, not singed in hell, but raised, and raised by his own power, victoriously, triumphantly, to the destruction of the last enemy, death.

Look him in the face in all these respects, of humiliation and of exaltation too. And then, as a picture looks at the one who looks at it, God, on whom you keep your eye, will keep God's eye on you. And, as in the creation, when God commanded light out of darkness but gave you a capacity for this light, and as in your calling, when God shines in your heart, God gave you a beginning of this light, so in associating yourself to God at the last day, God will perfect, consummate, accomplish all, and give you the light of the glory of God in the face of Christ Jesus there.

God will accomplish all.

Sources for the Readings

The weekday readings are based on the sermons as given in *The Sermons of John Donne* by George R. Potter and Evelyn M. Simpson. They are cited simply by volume and page. The prayers are drawn either from the same source or from *John Donne: Selections from Divine Poems, Sermons, Devotions, and Prayers* by John Booty. These are cited simply as "Booty" with a page number. The sonnets and other poems can be found in most collections of Donne's poetry and in most anthologies of Donne's work and, therefore, no specific citations are provided.

Ash Wednesday—vol. 10, p.74; vol. 1, pp. 248–249
Thursday after Ash Wednesday—vol. 1, pp. 190–192
Friday after Ash Wednesday—vol. 2, pp. 214–216
Saturday after Ash Wednesday—vol. 1, pp. 308–309

The First Sunday in Lent—vol. 8, p. 61
Monday in the First Week of Lent—vol. 8, pp. 222–224
Tuesday in the First Week of Lent—vol. 8, pp. 224–225
Wednesday in the First Week of Lent—vol. 3, pp. 358–359
Thursday in the First Week of Lent—vol. 8, pp. 226–228
Friday in the First Week of Lent—vol. 8, pp. 229–230
Saturday in the First Week of Lent—vol. 8, pp. 231–233

The Second Sunday in Lent—vol. 8, pp. 62–63
Monday in the Second Week of Lent —vol. 8, pp. 235–236
Tuesday in the Second Week of Lent—vol. 9, pp. 47–48
Wednesday in the Second Week of Lent—vol. 9, pp. 62–64
Thursday in the Second Week of Lent—vol. 8, pp. 140–142

Friday in the Second Week of Lent—vol. 4, pp. 148–149
Saturday in the Second Week of Lent—vol. 3, pp. 362–365

The Third Sunday in Lent—Booty, pp. 291–292
Monday in the Third Week of Lent—vol. 4, pp. 149–151
Tuesday in the Third Week of Lent—vol. 2, pp. 294–296
Wednesday in the Third Week of Lent—vol. 1, pp. 180–181
Thursday in the Third Week of Lent—vol. 6, pp. 198–201
Friday in the Third Week of Lent—vol. 9, pp. 296-298, 303–304
Saturday in the Third Week of Lent—vol. 5, pp. 280–281

The Fourth Sunday in Lent—Booty, pp. 297–299
Monday in the Fourth Week of Lent—vol. 10, pp. 134–139
Tuesday in the Fourth Week of Lent—vol. 8, pp. 370–372
Wednesday in the Fourth Week of Lent—vol. 4, pp. 73–74;
      vol. 1, p. 302
Thursday in the Fourth Week of Lent—vol. 6, pp. 170–172
Friday in the Fourth Week of Lent—vol. 7, pp. 68–70
Saturday in the Fourth Week of Lent—vol. 9, pp. 213 ff.

The Fifth Sunday in Lent—Booty, p. 283–284
Monday in the Fifth Week of Lent—vol. 9, pp. 213 ff.
Tuesday in the Fifth Week of Lent—vol. 5, pp. 270–272, 278
Wednesday in the Fifth Week of Lent—vol. 7, pp. 264–265;
      vol. 7, p. 311; vol. 2, pp. 149–150
Thursday in the Fifth Week of Lent—vol. 7, pp. 268–269;
      vol. 10, pp. 72–73
Friday in the Fifth Week of Lent—vol. 9, pp. 126–127;
Saturday in the Fifth Week of Lent—vol. 3, p. 280;
      vol. 7, pp. 232–233; vol. 9, pp. 75–76

Palm Sunday—Booty, pp. 292–293
Monday in Holy Week—vol. 5, pp. 266–267
Tuesday in Holy Week—vol. 2, pp. 197–200

Wednesday in Holy Week—vol. 3, pp. 202–204
Maundy Thursday—vol. 10, pp. 245–247
Good Friday—vol. 10, pp. 247–248
Easter Even—vol. 9, pp. 104–108

Easter Day—vol. 8, p. 191
Monday in Easter Week—vol. 8, pp. 80–82
Tuesday in Easter Week—vol. 7, pp. 69–71
Wednesday in Easter Week—vol. 9, pp. 127–129
Thursday in Easter Week—vol. 4, pp. 87–88, 128
Friday in Easter Week—vol. 4, p. 129
Saturday in Easter Week—vol. 4, pp. 129–130

For Further Reading

Bald, R.C. *John Donne, A Life.* Oxford: Clarendon Press, 1970. The only recent biography, although much biographical material is contained in the introductions to all the following.

Booty, John. *John Donne: Selections from Divine Poems, Sermons, Devotions, and Prayers.* New York and Mahwah: Paulist Press, 1990. A good selection of Donne's theological work. Most of the Latin references are removed and spelling is modernized. Nearly complete texts of eight sermons are provided. One of the sermons (drawn from Potter and Simpson's volumes) is incorrectly identified.

Carey, John. *John Donne: A Critical Edition of the Major Works.* Oxford and New York: Oxford University Press, 1990. Selections from Donne's secular prose and poetry, as well as the sacred. The spelling is modernized but some of the Latin references are retained. There are brief excerpts from many of the sermons but the complete text only of "Death's Duel," Donne's last and best-known sermon.

Potter, George R. and Evelyn M. Simpson. *The Sermons of John Donne.* Berkeley and Los Angeles: University of California Press, 1953–1962. These ten volumes contain all of Donne's sermons with much introductory material to analyze the sermons and set them in context.

Webber, Joan. *Contrary Music: The Prose Style of John Donne.* Madison, Wisconsin: University of Wisconsin Press, 1964. This is a study of the sources and structure of Donne's prose, especially as it was developed in his preaching.